MY FAVORITE HORROR MOVIE 2

The New Blood

EDITED & CURATED BY

CHRISTIAN ACKERMAN, FELISSA ROSE & CHUCK FOSTER

Published by
Black Vortex Cinema
1800 N. La Brea
Los Angeles, CA 90046

INTERIOR LAYOUT/COVER PHOTO: CHRISTIAN ACKERMAN
COVER DESIGN: JOSH MCKEVITT
JOSHMCKEVITT.COM

JOIN US!

WEB:
BLACKVORTEXCINEMA.COM

FACEBOOK/INSTAGRAM:
@MYFAVORITEHORRORMOVIE

TWITTER:
@MYFAVEHORROR

ISBN: 978-1-7322702-2-0

Dedicated to my friend
Sid Haig.
A man of endless talent.

-Felissa

BODY PARTS

INTRODUCTION

BY

CHUCK FOSTER

For the most part, horror movies are dismissed by "serious" critics and theatergoers as vulgar exploitation pandering to the lowest common denominator. To them, things that go bump in the night simply don't exist, so indulging in superstitions is just a stupid waste of time.

Every hardcore horror fan knows the anxiety that comes with admitting to a stranger that these films full of ghosts, gore and girls are your main form of entertainment. It's one step away from saying you like porn. Most people react with a scowl or proclaim that they get scared too easily to watch "those" movies. You're better off not bringing up cinema at all lest your coworkers, or that person you met on a dating app, or the random guy you talk to at the bar all think you're some kind of pervert because you enjoy watching scantily clad, or fully nude, teenagers get dismembered in the woods by some maniac with a garden tool.

This is why horror is such a small, tight-knit community. When we encounter one of our own, we feel a sense of kinship and we build relationships based on our mutual love for this universally maligned genre. We go to conventions to rub shoulders with like-minded individuals and, even though we may never actually talk to most of them, we know that we are all there to share in our mutual love of that one thing that binds us together.

Most of the people in this book have made horror a living, if not a lifestyle. Sure you'll read "to be honest, I don't really like horror movies," but they wouldn't be here if that were the case. Every single essay within these pages has been written by someone whose life was changed - for the better - because a single horror movie came into their lives. These folks are dedicated to their craft, mission, purpose, whatever they want to call it, and they all know they wouldn't be where they are without that one spark that ignited their futures.

All forms of entertainment, be it books, music or film, exist for the sole purpose of escapism. We in the horror community prefer to escape into the fears and nightmares that haunt us every day. It's the reason I read paranormal message boards before going to sleep, then see how far I can make it across my cozy NYC apartment without turning on the lights.

Personally speaking, I've never been prouder to be part of anything in my life. Being asked to take part in the first book was an honor (Dawn of the Dead near the end), but being asked to curate and edit the sequels, well, that's an ordained knighthood that just makes me blush. I haven't met most of the contributors in this book, but I know they are my people, just like you are for reading it.

NIGHT OF THE CREEPS

BY

MICHAEL VARRATI

Filmmaker, Screenwriter, Host

Tales of Poe, Deathcember, Dead for Filth

Twitter: @MichaelVarrati

To me, horror has always been the most powerful of genres. By its very definition, it's a mechanism of subversion and quite often the embodiment of otherness. At its best, horror can be a great tool of social commentary, taking the things we may not be ready to face and wrapping them up in a monster that we can process and watch it disappear with the roll of the end credits. It's a cathartic medium. It can be funny. It can be challenging. It can push our boundaries and make us reevaluate the ones we live within.

As such, to be a horror fan can sometimes be an embarrassment of riches. To move within a genre that the world at large so often eschews, it's like we're privy to a secret that is all our own. These movies are our release, our escape, and occasionally our therapy.

...and if you feel on the outside, even doubly so. For those marginalized or othered by society at large, horror can often seem like a reflection. We can look at the plight of the Creature from the Black Lagoon or Frankenstein's Monster and know what it's like to be rejected by the crowd. We can watch as Laurie Strode so desperately yearns to just be like the other girls, and sympathize with her longing.

Horror is powerful, because at its core, horror is personal.

As such, for ardent horror fans, it can sometimes be difficult to choose a favorite film. We may have the ones that have more significant impact than others, but when you've invested so much passion into the genre...it's also likely that you've attached different emotions and memories to different films.

Even so...there's always that one you return to...the horror movie that feels the most you.

But, bearing all that in mind, before I can fully explain what that particular movie is for me, I do need to tell you about another one first. Why? Because of all the things horror can be, it's also very much a journey.

When I was a kid, I was what the textbooks would classically define as a "scaredy cat." I had no interest in anything threatening, frightening, or at all spooky. I avoided any and all material that veered into darker territory and frequently policed my own content far more rigidly than my parents ever attempted. In fact, my mom and dad love to tell the story that I was so concerned with scary content that I would often run over and turn off the TV at the first tinge of a dramatic shift in music that might suggest anything ominous. This had to be very vexing for my parents, as I'm sure they just wanted to watch their programs after a long day of work.

I made it very clear early on: This kind of funny business was not for me. No how. No way. No questions.

...or so I thought.

One rather unremarkable day, I was perusing the *TV Guide* (remember those?) and happened upon a listing for a program called *USA Up All Night* that was going to be hosting a double feature of a movie called *Attack of the Killer Tomatoes* and its sequel.

I was transfixed. *Killer Tomatoes*? What did that mean? How could tomatoes be anything but pizza topping or a sandwich accessory? Obsession quickly seized my little brain and I insisted, begged, and pleaded to be granted the opportunity to see what all this produce-themed mayhem was about.

Now, my mom, having lived through several occasions where I scared the hell out of myself with some mundane content, was definitely dubious. However, she didn't want to fully censor my curiosity, so she agreed that I could stay up and watch the double feature with the caveat that she was going to watch with me (I assume to make sure I didn't have a complete meltdown).

When the night arrived, the movie started, and my mom promptly fell asleep 15 minutes in. But I hardly noticed. I was enraptured. These tomatoes weren't scary. They were outrageous. Crazy. And so much fun. I wasn't scared. I was in love.

Back then, how *Up All Night* used to structure their screenings was that they'd show both movies with the host, Rhonda Shear, and then when the program ended, they'd just keep playing the movies back to back until sun-up or infomercials took over. With my mom fast asleep on the couch and my attention fully given to this silliness in front of me, I must've stayed up all night, watching both those movies several times in a row.

By the time morning came, I was born anew. A horror fan birthed in the aftermath of tomato carnage. My mom was worried that I wouldn't be able to handle watching the movies, but I don't think she could have ever planned they'd change my life.

Now, I fully recognize that *Attack of the Killer Tomatoes* and its subsequent sequels (*Killer Tomatoes Eat France* is a veritable masterpiece) are hardly hardcore horror and veer more into comedic camp than anything. But you have to understand, that evening introduced me to a fundamental shift in my perception. What I witnessed were movies unlike any I was seeing at the local multiplex or on the channels all my friends were watching. I became aware that there was something else out there…a strange underground where movies could be so much more and be so much weirder.

…and I didn't know why at the time, but I knew I wanted that…I wanted the weird, I wanted to find the movies that were too strange for the multiplex. The outsiders of cinema felt like home, because in some ways they felt like me.

I know it sounds bizarre to say, but with that single night of viewing, I felt like a scaredy cat no more. Instead, I became hungry…and for more than just tomatoes. I wanted to know about the renegade movies that made me feel more myself. I wanted to dive in and explore all that entailed. And if that meant blood and guts, ghosts and ghouls, I was ready. I wanted to face the things I was afraid of and wrap myself up in them. The movies that once made me run and turn the TV off became the things that would keep me glued to the screen.

USA Up All Night continued to be my gateway, which eventually led to Stephen King and later *The X-Files*. But those early days of horror on cable felt triumphant. The world would go to bed and I was discovering the likes of Freddy and Jason for the first time. *Scream* hadn't happened yet and horror was in an alleged downswing, so these movies that I was seeing felt like they were all mine. Kids at school wanted to talk about football and I wanted to theorize about how Michael Myers was going to return in the next *Halloween*. Honestly, I didn't think it could get any better.

…and then I found *Night of the Creeps*.

I was born in the early '80s, which means that I while I was relatively young for the tail end of the decade, the monolithic pop culture benchmarks of the time were still very much present in my world; when it came to movies, it meant the likes of Steven Spielberg, Robert Zemeckis, and John Hughes. Blockbusters with space aliens and heartfelt dramedies with cool teens navigating their lives were the order of the day. You wanted to be Marty McFly or Ferris Bueller and have a grand adventure, even while you were finding yourself.

Except, I didn't.

While I appreciated those movies, I never quite felt like Marty was me. I related far more to Ally Sheedy in *The Breakfast Club* than I ever did Ferris or Emilio Estevez. And though I knew I was an Ally, I wanted to be a Ferris...because that's what we were told to want. So, in a way, I suppose I was having my own little John Hughes crisis while trying to relate to John Hughes.

I didn't see *Night of the Creeps* when it first debuted in 1986. I was still too young. But, as with most of my horror intake, I caught it a few years later when it hit the late night cable circuit. Instantly, there was a tone that clicked. A tone that was familiar.

The story of a nerdy guy and his even nerdier friend who take a chance to rush a frat at their college with the hopes of catching the attention of a popular girl felt like John Hughes. The heartache-drenched soliloquies of Chris, played with aplomb by Jason Lively, would have been right at home in *Sixteen Candles*...and the sassy retorts of his friend J.C., played by Steve Marshall, had all the makings of an Anthony Michael Hall or Alan Ruck embodied sidekick. In many respects, they were the personification of the quintessential '80s young adults: Full of yearning, self-doubt, and the need to be loved.

...and then the alien slugs show up. And the zombies.

...did I mention this movie also opens with an axe-wielding mental asylum escapee?

Written and directed by Fred Dekker, who also gave us cult classic *The Monster Squad* and would later go on to pen a Predator flick, *Night of the Creeps* is a genius exercise in genre, because in many ways, it straddles several genres. I always evoke John Hughes when doing a deep dive on this film, because in an era where teens were so frequently presented as stock stereotypes, Hughes sought to humanize and give pathos to his characters, which in turn made teenagers and young adults of the era feel like they were finally being seen. Horror, as much as

I love it, was often one of the biggest offenders of creating one dimensional teens to fulfill a body count. It became an expected and rote trope to introduce characters just to see them die. While that certainly has its place within the genre, it also made for a lot of interchangeable moments in films that weren't as artfully curated. Yet here was Dekker, taking the time to make sure we connected with the characters, imbuing them with that same level of pathos, and ensuring we couldn't help but feel in some way that Chris and J.C. were us just trying to make it in the world.

Of course, as aforementioned, Chris and J.C.'s youthful follies are not all that this movie is about. In the world of the film, it's established that 30 years before our heroes' university stay, a pod carrying malicious alien slugs crash landed on Earth, allowing the slimy creatures to hop into the body of a curious college student, even as his date gets hacked and slashed by an escaped mental patient. The cops arrive, the bodies are discovered, and our slug infested co-ed is put on ice.

Fast-forward to present day (well, 1986). Chris and J.C. are attempting to rush a frat so that Chris can impress a girl. The frat, with no intention of actually letting the two friends in, sends them on a fool's errand to go to the university's medical center to bring back a research cadaver. They claim it's a prank that will earn them cred, and then...and only then...would they be considered for fraternity brotherhood.

Through a series of comedic events, Chris and J.C. stumble upon a body in deep freeze and accidentally thaw it out. However, as you might have guessed, that's the body with the slugs...and now that they're awake...they're ready to cause a little chaos. Add to the fact that a dead person who's infested by a slug can still move around, and you suddenly have a recipe for alien mayhem with a heaping helping of zombified coeds out for blood.

As far as plot goes, you know everything you need to know: Two college friends are just trying their best to get by in life & love when alien slugs show up and raise the dead, leading to a fight for survival on an otherwise posh American college campus. It's the kind of logline that seems patently absurd and perfectly suited for drive-in fare.

Yet, *Night of the Creeps* is more than just its logline or the details of its plot. What makes this movie a success is the characters.

Beyond Chris and J.C., perhaps the film's most central character, if not its most outwardly identifiable, is Detective Ray Cameron, brought to life by '80s man's man Tom Atkins. Haunted by his past (does it have something to do with that initial slug-infused axe murder? Of course it does), Cameron begrudgingly takes on one last case, only to find himself thrust face-to-face with the thing he'd been running from all those years.

While Atkins infuses with Cameron with the expected level of machismo, there's also a fragility that is present that provides the character layers. Though Cameron, constantly delivering his cool catchphrase "Thrill Me," is intentionally presented as the epitome of '80s action hero archetypes, through Dekker's careful craftsmanship and Atkin's intelligent portrayal, he becomes so much more.

Cameron's story becomes one of loss and longing, and in many ways, runs parallel with Chris's own sense of yearning in the present day. Though fundamentally different people, Cameron and Chris are united by not only their need to survive the night, but on a deeper level, a need to connect with a world they both are trying to find their place within.

...and even as Cameron and Chris grapple with their past and present respectively, J.C. seemingly is having a crisis of longing of his own.

From the very beginning, J.C.'s motivations are always for Chris's betterment. It's clear from the get-go that J.C. has little interest in the frat, but chooses to rush because he believes it will make Chris happy. In fact, throughout the movie, J.C. takes on a lot of burdens to ensure that Chris gets what he wants, and when the duo final have a tense moment about it,

J.C. reminds Chris that everything he's done has been in service to his friend.

Unfortunately (spoiler alert), *Night of the Creeps* is not an endeavor that J.C. is destined to survive. But his passing is unlike many in horror movies of the era. He's not presented merely as fodder for a body count, he's the emotional core of the movie...and it's his caring that eventually spurs Chris to take up arms and fight back.

There's a pivotal moment in *Night of the Creeps* where Chris finds a posthumous recorded message from J.C., who used his final breaths to make a video to not only inform his friend how to fight back against the slugs...but to lay his feelings bare.

There's been some critical discourse back and forth about the nature and coding of this scene, and whether Dekker had a larger intent for J.C.'s final message. For me, the intent was immaterial. The message was clear: J.C. loved Chris. He said so.

Some may argue that because J.C.'s sexual orientation is never directly defined in the film with any specific terminology or labels, this scene is up for debate. That perhaps J.C.'s profession of love was merely that of the love between friends in one's final moments.

...and maybe that's so.

But let me tell you this much: When I was a kid seeing this movie for the first time, to have a moment where a boy who was not all that much older than me get to earnestly and unabashedly tell his friend he loved him...and for that to have emotional impact...that meant something. Because when I was a kid, that wasn't done. Not in movies. And definitely not in life.

Then, to reflect back on the fact that J.C.'s entire motivation throughout his short cinematic existence was to ensure the happiness of the person he loved, even if it meant sacrificing his own, that felt powerful, poignant, and real.

Because that's what happens when you're an Ally Sheedy in a world of Emilios. You sacrifice who you are to maintain the status quo. You help other people get their happy ending, because the world doesn't approve of or guarantee yours. At least that's what we were led to believe.

...and here was a movie laying it bare in front of us. In the middle of alien slugs and zombie frat boys was an earnest moment of queerness. Of otherness. And that's what horror does best. It gives voice to the other, even if sometimes unintentionally.

Ultimately, that's why I love *Night of the Creeps*...because it both encapsulates a moment in time, but also transcends it using genre as the gateway. My appreciation for this movie goes far beyond J.C.'s profession for Chris. In some ways, that's barely scratching the surface. This film is a full smorgasbord of what horror can and should be. There's an intergenerational story of longing across the years. There's the innocence and complications of young love. There's what happens when we are faced with insurmountable challenges that force us to discover who we really are.

...and there's alien slugs. Zombies. Axe muderers. And one amazing sequence with flamethrowers that still makes me giddy as a child.

Also, it's just cool.

By taking the sensibilities of the '50s drive-in era and imbuing them with the excess of the '80s, *Night of the Creeps* caters to two different decades and comes out feeling wholly unique. It's not just as if John Hughes had made a zombie movie. It's better.

It's a love letter and a statement all at once. In many ways, it's also exactly what that initial *Killer Tomatoes* viewing made me desire: a film that wears its otherness like a badge of pride. In a world where my peers had their movies, here was a movie that showed that you can be presented with impossible odds, whether they be from space or the grave, and that you're strong enough to take a stand, fight back, and become who you're supposed to be.

My peers had their movies, but this movie was mine. They wouldn't understand, and I didn't expect them to.

That's the thing, really. To the world outside, a movie with slugs from space and undead co-eds must seem silly. But to horror fans, we know between those lines it can also be empowering.

When I discovered that initial night that there was a world of movies beyond those at the multiplex, I was excited because I was delving into something I didn't know. What I didn't realize at the time is that what I actually was discovering was myself. I found my place in horror movies not because of fear, but because horror movies show we can overcome it and become stronger. More so, they teach us the inherent value in the unusual, the strange, and odd…and how sometimes those things are also our beauty and our strength.

I was and remain attracted to *Night of the Creeps* because it in many ways exemplifies all of these tenants. It tells the story of a kid who has to fight back against the night to become who he wants to be, a man who has to come to terms with who he was, and a boy who maybe, just maybe, looked life in the face, stood a little taller, and wore his heart on his sleeve. That the movie also treats us to magnificent monsters, harrowing circumstances, and amazing one-liners, is just icing on the cake.

Night of the Creeps does what horror ought, it thrills. But it also leaves us with something more. It bucks the norm to show us that often the norm isn't all it's cracked up to be.

Now, perhaps in invoking the name of a film that is widely regarded for its comedic properties, you're slightly surprised that I express my appreciation for it with such a serious lens. But, it's as I said at the beginning: horror is a genre of subverting expectations and digging beneath the surface to reveal and reflect. For me, *Night of the Creeps* is a movie that brings joy, but also empowerment. It's a reminder we can be many things, but we are most powerful when we are earnestly and unabashedly ourselves.

That's not a lesson easily learned. It took me many years of self-reflection, *Killer Tomatoes*, and alien slugs to finally accept it to be true. When I think of this movie, I think of all the reasons I love horror, and why I know it makes us stronger.

Horror is the most powerful genre, but we're the ones who give it power. We quiver at its monsters and invest in its heroes, all the while knowing that what we're really seeing are parts of ourselves. Sometimes it's a reflection we're not always ready for, but in some ways that's the best part. That's why we're horror fans. We want to see anyway.

Like Tom Atkins, we stare at the otherness...because we are the otherness...and issue the challenge: "Thrill me."

...and you know? I hope it does. Bring on the slugs. Bring on the zombies.

Cause that's who I am, and I wouldn't want it any other way.

THE EXORCIST

BY

CAMILLA JACKSON

Actress/Filmmaker/Creative Director
Los Angeles Overnight, *Arena Cinelounge*,
Cinelounge Presents Podcast
Instagram: @TheCamillaJackson
ArenaScreen.com Cinelounge.Libsyn.com

I was about six years old when my brother informed me that the small birthmark on the left side of my neck resembled the number 666. Of course, at that age I was unsure what that number even represented, but I had a feeling from his delivery that it was nefarious.

I was too scared to even look at it in the mirror. It was the dirty little secret I kept hidden behind my blonde locks, my albatross, my cross to bear.

From then on, it was my mission to find out more about what this dreaded birthmark meant for me and my future, and the best route for my investigation was through movies. I aimed to provide myself with education on all things Satan, possession, and the dark arts. After all, knowledge is power, and I was going to need a lot of that to go head-to-head with Beelzebub.

With the understanding that I was in some way affiliated with the Antichrist, I concluded that he inevitably was going to have a demon inhabit my body to carry out his work. The thought of becoming possessed consumed me. There was one time that I had left an old sandwich under my bed, and soon a swarm of flies and maggots appeared all over my window like a quilt of Muscidae - exactly like in 1979's *The Amityville Horror.* I was doomed for sure.

It didn't make things easier that, for some reason, my mother, whose only knowledge of "Genesis" was limited to Phil Collins, sent me to a hardcore Catholic school. I knew God would be mad that this "marked" and unbaptized child consumed the bread and wine at Mass, but there was a small amount of comfort in knowing that Satan would approve of my anarchistic disposition.

One day in class, we were made to watch a video of an exorcism. It was amazing. I had to see and know more.

I can recall my father watching a great British anthology series in the '80s called *Hammer House of Horror*, which had more than a few episodes that touched on the occult. I would listen to it through the wall late at night and hang on his every word when he would tell me about it the next day.

In some individuals, fear can create a chemical reaction in the brain that mimics the feeling of excitement, and I most definitely fell into that category. Like a gruesome accident scene that you can't look away from, I was drawn to the dark side like a magnet.

Around the age of 10, I heard murmurings about a film called *The Exorcist* and asked my father if we could rent it. He was thrilled. We watched it. I had to hide my intense fear, for I was a proud child, but oh boy, I had found it: the film that epitomized my fate! I was Regan! It was around this time that I happened upon some literature that said that prepubescent girls were most susceptible to possession, and this is when my horror movie watching stepped up a notch. I needed to be informed. With enough research, I would be able to combat the evil inside me.

By the age of 15 I had summoned up enough courage to look at the birthmark on my neck in a mirror - it wasn't a 666! It was a simple blob. If I had to compare it to anything, it would be more like the *Millenium Falcon*. Nothing sinister here. My brother had lied!

I was relieved for sure, but I was on a roll with this horror movie thing. I no longer needed to watch for survival reasons, but I could view it for pleasure.

I ran the gamut at the local Video Ezy, renting all manner of horror, from favorites such as *Blood Sucking Freaks* to *Terrorvision*, and of course, the *Nightmare on Elm Street* franchise rocked my world.

Technically, my favorite film is *Evil Dead II* - it is superb. Such inventive filmmaking, and Bruce Campbell is one of a kind, but as I write this, I realize that it is *The Exorcist* that has had the most impact on me. The one film that still truly scares me, which is important.

These days, it's virtually impossible for a film to spook me, and I am on an eternal quest to experience the feeling that I hate but love so much. Surprisingly, I miss it. Occasionally, moments in a film almost take me there, but I still long for the days of being consumed with fear. Not being able to go to the bathroom by myself is where it's at. Watching a horror film that gnaws at something within and puts you in a state of being genuinely freaked out is an experience of real human emotion. It's experiential, visceral and, above all, damn entertaining - and it stays with you for days.

Thankfully, I have not been possessed, but I am still on the hunt for a new film that can make me believe that I will be.

NIGHT OF THE LIVING DEAD

(1968)

BY

LARRY ROSS

Horror Film Lover, Collectibles Dealer

Blast From The Past

Facebook: @Lawrence.W.Ross.9 @BlastFromThePastInc

BlastFromThePast.tv

I'm a 55 year old man today, but my first brush with *Night of the Living Dead* came as a youngster of around seven or eight years of age. We were visiting relatives in the small (microscopic) town of Driggs, Idaho, and there wasn't much to do in the evenings. They had even fewer channels than we did in Los Angeles and LA only got seven in those days. To combat the boredom, I was thumbing through my grandmother's old copies of Reader's Digest, reading the rarely funny jokes and the occasional article that caught my eye when I came across Roger Ebert's review of George Romero's 1968 seminal zombie film *Night of the Living Dead*. I was already a budding monster fanatic, having recently accomplished the Herculean task of watching ALL of *Horror of Dracula* (without leaving the room, no matter how scary it got, except for that one part which didn't count). Anyway, after delivering a detailed plot synopsis, Ebert mostly talked about how scary the movie was, how devastated the kids at the matinee were, including a description of one crying little girl and how the new ratings system might go a long way towards protecting kids from such intense viewing experiences. (Author's note: I've recently tracked down and reread Ebert's review. He's much kinder to the film than I'd remembered, although he does provide an INEXCUSABLE number of spoilers, including the ending.) In a nutshell, the movie is about a group of people who have taken refuge in a farmhouse from a growing army of reanimated corpses. As time goes by and hope wains, tensions within the group mount. What got to me most was the sense of hopelessness that the characters experienced in the face of the mounting horde of the undead.

The next time I encountered the film, I was 13 in the grocery store. It was pretty much standard practice to spend my time at the spinning rack of paperback books while mom did the shopping. I've never forgotten how creeped out I was by that review all those years ago and suddenly there it was: a novelization of the movie. The cover depicted pale hands clutching their way through a partially boarded up window (there's a copy of the exact edition available on eBay right now for a mere $75). I picked it up, read the blurb on the back, and then thumbed through the photos in the center. Now I had photographic images to go with the ones that had been chasing around in my head for the past five years or so. I knew what Ben looked like, as well as Barbara, Johnny, Mr. and Mrs. Cooper...and...THEM. The dead. Oddly, they looked both more frightening and, yet somehow, more ordinary than I'd expected. But there were so many. That was the true horror: there were so many you just couldn't hope to eliminate them all. I was getting more and more of a sense of just how futile the fight against the ghoulish mass would be. Needless to say, I didn't sleep well that night.

It would be a few more years before I actually saw the film.

It was screened by a local station in Los Angeles on a late late show. By this time, I was in high school, and despite nearly ten years of building it up in my mind, I instantly became obsessed by it, which is even more impressive when you take the film's miniscule budget of only around $7000 into account. I'd regularly rent the video with friends and I'd watch it over and over, memorizing the lines and inserting them into my daily speech. "Kill the brain and you kill the ghoul." "Yeah, they're dead... they're all messed up." "Good shot. Ok, he's dead. Let's go get him. That's another one for the fire." And of course the classic: "They're coming to get you Barbara." It used to drive my mom crazy.

It's genuinely scary. The grainy film quality instills the feeling that you're watching an old documentary. The performances, while uneven, are generally pretty good. Duane Jones' portrayal of Ben is particularly well defined. Frightened, determined, heroic and ultimately wrong (turns out the cellar WAS the safest place all along). Also worth mentioning is Judith O'Dea's Barbara. I'm not sure how much of what we see was due to her acting and how much Romero's direction deserves credit, but it's one of the only times I can think of where a character that's experienced a trauma isn't required to simply brush it off and move on. Following the death of her brother in the first scene, she essentially goes into shock and pretty much stays there for the rest of the movie. The final performance that I'd like to bring up is that of Ken Hardman's Mr. Cooper. He's a snarling, selfish, cowardly opponent to Ben, but oddly, he's not a racist. Given the country's social/political climate at the time, we would expect Mr. Cooper to bring up Ben's ethnicity as a negative. He never does. Romero has stated many times that Jones was cast for no other reason than his skills as an actor and there was no political statement being made. It hasn't stopped critics from claiming that Romero was saying something more regarding race in America. In fact, the number of film analysts that have tried to find a deeper meaning in the fact that Ben is African American rivals the crowd of zombies outside the farmhouse. (Now THAT'S a movie I'd want to see: "Critics vs. Zombies.") Interestingly, by the time he made *Dawn of the Dead* a decade later, Romero didn't hesitate to embrace an underlying commentary on mindless consumerism. He did this by setting the film in a mall that zombies continue to want to enter - long after their ability to use the products they desire had vanished.

There's really no way to talk about the impact that *Night of the Living Dead* had on me without discussing the ending. As the sole survivor, Ben carefully creeps back upstairs when he hears approaching rescuers. Peering out a window he's mistaken for one of the dead and is shot through the forehead by a member of the redneck posse. The guy we've been rooting for throughout the movie, our hero, is killed because of a stupid mistake. Pointless. Meaningless. Just like any other accident. The moment lands like a gut punch. Even though I knew it was coming, I wanted to shout at the screen because of the unfairness of it. I still kind of do, but it's that very unfairness that makes the film so powerful.

Night of the Living Dead was the first modern zombie film. As such, its cultural influence cannot be overstated. The number of films that have been inspired by Romero's classic are legion. Just as Nosferatu was the first vampire film to introduce the idea that sunlight is deadly to vampires, Night was the first to establish many of the concepts that we take for granted in a zombie film. A few examples: zombies must be shot in the head or otherwise have their brain destroyed in order to be stopped; zombies eat living people; zombies create other zombies by killing the living; zombies are essentially without thought; zombies are slow; and, just like *The Terminator*, zombies will not stop, ever.

If you'd like further evidence of just how influential *Night of the Living Dead* (and its sequels) have become, just ask any serious horror fan what his plan for the zombie apocalypse is, and it's a safe bet they actually have one.

TREMORS

BY

BUZ WALLICK

Producer/Director
Twinsanity, Her Last Will, One of Us,
Never Sleep Again: The Elm Street Legacy, Psycho Granny
Twitter: @BuzDanger

Anyone who knows me would most likely assume my favorite horror film is *Jaws*, and they would be correct in that assumption. So why am I writing this essay on something else? Well, what could I possibly say about *Jaws* that hasn't already been said? The answer is nothing. So I've decided to go with a more underrated personal favorite. Something that deserves its day in the sun.

I'm talking about the *Jaws* of the desert: *Tremors.*

As I sit here writing this essay - listening to the excellent *Tremors* score no less - I keep asking myself why I hold this movie in such high regard? Well, there are plenty of reasons I'm sure, but it's never been a film I've analyzed with friends over drinks, or discussed in film courses, or any of the other multitude of situations where cinephiles openly discuss great cinema. In fact, I doubt *Tremors* ever enters into the lexicon of greatest movies ever…yet it absolutely should be. I'm going to prove to you, with science and reason, why *Tremors* is the best horror movie ever. Or at least my favorite horror movie.

Much like how at first glance *Jaws* is just a silly B-movie about an island town being attacked by a shark, *Tremors* is just a silly B-movie about giant worms attacking a small desert town. Yet both films are elevated from that simple pitch. Not to go into too many comparisons (too late), but I believe the biggest way these films advance this material is characters, characters, and more characters.

A movie is only ever as good as its leads, and that's what sets *Tremors* apart. Val and Earl are two average-to-lower intelligence handymen, determined to escape their lives in Perfection, Nevada even if it means turning down a six pack for work. Rhonda, a grad student with some wits about her quickly becomes the expert on how to handle GIANT MAN EATING WORMS, even though she has no experience in handling GIANT MAN EATING WORMS. And then of course there is none other than Burt "Don't tell me the Cold War is over" Gummer, brilliantly played by Michael Gross. There are plenty of other supporting players too, all great in their own right (except for Melvin, because screw Melvin).

These characters are all given full life from the actors portraying them. They have lives, things have happened to them before and things will happen to them after (a few of them anyways). They feel like real people, not just worm food.

That's a big deal for me when it comes to characters. There is nothing worse than people who are just in the movie to complete a task and then die. It's boring.

Not the case in *Tremors*. You learn to care about these people. You want to see them succeed, and there is this weird sort of human pride thing going on where you want these rednecks with average intelligence to prove that they are smarter than the Graboids.

Speaking of Graboids, let's talk about the outstanding special effects in *Tremors*, created by the good folks over at Amalgamated Dynamics (*Starship Troopers, Mars Attacks, Alien 3*). These guys studied under the great Stan Winston and it shows! The Graboid FX in the film are a healthy mix of resized worms as well as seamless miniature work. For instance, the rec room basement attack is a miniature Graboid mixed with footage of the Gummers using every piece of ammo they have at their disposal. The animatronic effects work so well that, like our characters, the Graboids feel like real animals. Not to mention the sound design also makes them threatening and real. Honestly, there are few monster movies like this in which the movie takes such great care to make them feel like "real" animals. The science, while made up, is plausible and makes sense. And everyone takes the Graboids seriously. They are never played for laughs. The characters themselves are funny, but not the worms. This is perfectly encapsulated with the death of (SPOILERS) Walter Chang. The gang comically scrambles to turn off a loud ice machine only to be too late and the Graboids burst through the floor and eat poor old Walter Chang. And it's played deadly seriously, affecting our characters' emotions and future decisions.

All of this owes itself to the brilliant script, written by Brent Maddock and S.S. Wilson, who took great care to create a living world. Everything is set up and knocked down. The script has everything from thrills and chills to laughs and romance. If you want to learn how to write a great horror film, read the script for *Tremors*. Great characters and a perfect structure.

So, going back to my earlier point, *Tremors* should absolutely be discussed in the pantheon of great horror. It has everything you could ever want in a movie and is a big reason why I love monster movies and horror so much. It is an excellent film that will forever be my favorite horror movie.

'Can you fly sucker?'

THE FLY (1986)

BY

GAVIN WILLIAMS

Writer, Director, Filmmaker
Await Further Instructions,
Chromophobia, Sleepworking, Hush
GavinWilliams.info Twitter: @Gavstatic

"Have you ever heard of insect politics? Neither have I. Insects...don't have politics. They're very...brutal. No compassion, no compromise. We can't trust the insect. I'd like to become the first...insect politician." - Seth Brundle

I have a confession.

I was never a horror fan growing up.

Well, perhaps, more accurately, I didn't know I was a horror fan.

As a kid, science fiction was my world, heavily influenced by my dad and a houseful of bright-spined paperbacks with captivatingly weird covers by artists such as Jim Burns and Chris Foss. I was exactly the right age to be consumed by the *Star Wars* Mania of the '70s and '80s, and everything that came along with it (comics, minifigs, novelisations, and tsunami of other questionable spinoffery).

My parents didn't really approve of horror, but they weren't weirdly militant about the subject, either. As lovely, mild, middle-class teachers, it just wasn't their thing. They didn't exactly forbid, though I do recall an episode of the (to modern eyes) quaintly tame Bill Bixby/Lou Ferrigno *Incredible Hulk* TV series being briskly switched off to save my younger brother suffering "nightmares" (in fairness, he was very young, and did have nightmares even without being traumatised by a former Mr. Universe in pea-green body makeup bellowing out of the screen).

So, I wasn't a horror fan. But there were always...hints...

Like something beneath the surface, bubbling, slowly festering, growing...

Well, I don't need to tell YOU.

You're all familiar with that kind of story, even if I wasn't back then.

For instance, of those bright-spined covers, the one that's burned most powerfully into my memory featured a blindingly white human skull framed by the dark arc of its space helmet. Similarly, I remember once browsing bookshelves on a shopping trip with my mum, and being drawn to a "grown-up" novel about a man who, after some experimental procedure or other, is afflicted by "melting skin" and goes on a rampage. Why? To get more skin? Who knows? Not I, because my mother firmly said she wasn't going to buy it for me...more nightmares saved, perhaps?

Furthermore, British kids TV of this period was, frankly, a bit untethered - surreal, seemingly unpoliced by even a whisper of "Won't someone think of the children!" style compliance - ambiguous, bat-shit, and frequently bone-chilling.

Series such as *King of the Castle* (allegorical fantasy head-fuck delving into a kid's broken mind after he falls down a lift shaft!), *Children of the Stones* (cryptic, spectral, time-rift horror sci-fi chiller set around a megalithic stone circle), and *The Owl Service* (a grimly haunting, psychosexual mythic possession ghost drama...thing), were filled with children deploying little more than a range of clipped British accents to confront horrifying manifestations of existential dread.

However, it's *Doctor Who* which sits atop this weird pile, and pretty much made me a writer. I was obsessed. I definitely started watching it way too early – at around three or four – and this was during the era where mad-eyed Tom Baker inhabited the titular role, and the production team was gleefully committed to producing a full-on Gothic horror show...for kids!

There were giant green maggots (which were possibly responsible for my imaginary friend, a blind green worm called Blangerous who lived in the letter box), intelligent alien spiders, gargantuan vampires and Egyptian mummies (who were robots underneath the bandages), infectious extraterrestrial seed pods unearthed from the Antarctic permafrost in a junior league proto-version of *John Carpenter's The Thing*, and a rapacious race of space wasps who, as a way to invade the earth, laid their eggs in the sleeping bodies of humans in suspended animation capsules...Plus, many, many other examples...It was all delightfully awful!

Even though this was nominally science fiction - the safe place - it turned me into the quintessential kid hiding behind the sofa, daring glimpses from between fingers, or around a parent's flank, simultaneously both petrified and excited, unable to look away. It was the strangeness and intensity of the images which distorted my imagination then, and shapes the themes present in my work today.

So, was my love of the horrific always there, waiting – a dark inheritance revealed – OR was it a genuine, slow transformation? I'm not sure.

I've said that *Doctor Who* was the gateway, but it was never the classic monsters which got to me. I always thought the

Daleks, for instance, were faintly silly, never scary. No, it was the half-creatures that burrowed under my skin. Time and again, in stories of that period, a guest character would become contaminated by something monstrous. Then, during the first episode and, over the following six weekly instalments, they would slowly, agonisingly, inexorably become something else and lose their humanity. It was that inevitability which affected me. They always tried to hide the "change" from their colleagues, in the vain hope of a cure, yet there was never a reprieve. They were always a goner. The best you could hope for was heroic sacrifice before you surrendered your mind, utterly, to savage alien appetites!

This was what absolutely fucking terrified me.

Transformation. Mutation. Metamorphosis. Change.

Which brings us to our marquee feature, David Cronenberg's remake of jaunty 1950s horror curio, *The Fly*, which is anything but jaunty and an absolute stone-cold body horror classic, an operatic-yet-strangely-theatrical mad science holy fuck paean to human physical dissolution!

I think it's probably Cronenberg's masterpiece, the perfect inflection point between his loopy, biotrash early gems like *Rabid*, *The Brood* and *Scanners*, and the drier, grown up, awards-chatter later-era works such as *Spider*, *A Dangerous Method*, and even *Crash*. For me, *The Fly* coheres all of his directorial tics and obsessions into the most satisfying package – a package, of course, leaking off-white pus – in a way his other best works never quite manage with the same panache.

The Fly brought in a larger, more mainstream audience which the likes of *Videodrome* ("Long live the New Flesh!") never would and had them reaching for the popcorn bucket to throw up in...in a way his previous project – the chilly, stately *Deadzone* adaptation wasn't able to. He's made more mature films, but none as complete as this.

Unlike Brundlefly, it's the perfect Cronenbergian synthesis.

I saw the film on its original theatrical release at the wonderful Odeon cinema on Pilgrim Street in Newcastle upon Tyne in Northern England where I still live. Sadly, the cinema closed in 2002, and was finally demolished after – in a perfect horror twist – the derelict, once-gorgeous façade collapsed into the street in 2017, narrowly missing pedestrians. In its day however, it was an uncontested jewel. Opening in 1931 as The Paramount, it was widely viewed as one of the finest cinemas in Europe, an Art Deco palace with gilded light fittings, oil paintings, elaborate plasterwork, and ornate wrought iron balustrades, many of which survived, albeit in a charmingly faded form, into the '70s/'80s/'90s when I was visiting it, week in, week out (I vividly recall the echoing sounds of footsteps in the cavernous original marble bathrooms). This degraded grandeur was a perfect stage for the insanity of *The Fly* to unfold...

The Odeon's main auditorium was immense, originally intended to seat up to 2600 punters in that one space – compared to around 2700 in a multiplex of similar scale, but spread across 16 separate screens – and, when full, it really was something to experience, the perfect epitome of shared cinema, thousands of gleaming eyes in the dark, mesmerised by that towering panel of flickering illumination. Precisely what you want for a horror film, arguably the most immersive genre, and this was especially true of *The Fly*, which is the very definition of visceral.

Cronenberg conjures a mood of impending catastrophe even from the ambiguous title sequence, where seething dabs of light flutter like insects before actually resolving into human guests at a scientific meet and greet. The audience is buffeted along by Howard Shore's wonderfully plush, swooping, slightly hysterical score, and they just know they can feel how wrong this is going to go from those opening (wing)beats...

In spite of the apparent intimacy of the story – the lion's share of the film is simply three characters bouncing off each other in Seth Brundle's lab-cum-apartment – *The Fly* is packed with fifty-foot high widescreen boom-o-vision moments where you just go GAH!!! After Seth Brundle takes his first ill-fated telepod trip, there follows a relentless fusillade of rising bombardments of SHIT HE ALMOST TORE THAT GUY'S HAND OFF AT THE WRIST! and CHRIST HE'S MELTING THROUGH HIS ANKLE WITH MANFLY-VOMIT! and HOLY FUCK NOW THE BOTTOM OF HIS JAW ACCIDENTALLY CAME OFF!!!!

I remember stumbling out afterwards, frankly more than a little shell-shocked by the sensory and narrative overload. When I teach screenwriting, I often talk about the theory of Narrative Escalation. All successful screenplays – all stories, really – should escalate as they progress, emotionally or dramatically, never falling into repetition or diminishing their intensity as they advance...And, man alive, *The Fly* ramps UP to its climax like a jet engine powered by superheated plasma straight from the heart of a dying star, before ending on a patented Cronenbergian exploding skull which is both a "fuck yeah" gore shot and an intensely poignant and heartfelt grace note.

What I also love – and appreciate even more today – is how tight Cronenberg and Charles Edward Pogue's writing craft is throughout. The script is full of innovative riffs on its elegantly simple core ideas. For example, because Brundle transforms into a human-fly hybrid, he can no longer digest food normally, so has to spit caustic vomit to break sustenance down outside his body...which he then uses as a disgusting weapon to dissolve human flesh! Similarly, the Brundlefly transformation alters his voice...so his voice-operated computer interface stops working. These clever permutations allow the filmmakers to construct gut-wrenchingly suspenseful set-pieces, including the climactic sequence where a fully-mutated Brundlefly tries to combine himself with Geena Davis' Veronica (and their unborn baby) via the telepods, only to have John Getz's Stathis Borans intervene with a shotgun. But Brundefly still ends up teleporting...And the audience has no idea where he's gone...

Until the computer screen, with agonising slowness, ticks out his ghoulish fate...

"Fusion of Brundle...and telepod...successful."

The characterisation in *The Fly* is flecked with a myriad of smart and subtle details, like Brundle's Einsteinian strategy of wearing identical suits every day so he doesn't "have to expend any thought on what I want to wear." Typically for Cronenberg this is a controlled and cerebral narrative and, despite the graphic crazy on display, we are seeing a cool, immensely confident craftsman at work.

There are so many elements which make *The Fly* great, and it would take a far longer essay to dissect them all, but we can't move on without paying homage to the mind-blowing (literally) special makeup FX of Chris Walas and Stephan Dupuis who track Brundle's awful decline as, at first, he seems to disintegrate as if from a terrible disease (tapping his teeth with a pen causes them to fall out!), then starts to assume the form of the insect-human hybrid with all manner of vile pustules and skeletal ridges and transmuted tissue. Apparently, some of the fun, grosser effects were achieved with surprisingly mundane ingredients: Brundlefly's vomit was a simple concoction of honey, raw eggs and milk!

For all its exuberantly squishy excesses, however, *The Fly* is, at heart, a simple story of dangerous obsession, a romance and a tragedy at once, and it would be nothing without its amazing cast.

This is the ur-Jeff Goldblum performance which turned him into The Jeff Goldblum, a star, and, eventually, the beloved meme-factory we know today. He makes the character arrogant yet sympathetic, naive and gawky, yet absolutely sells the sinewy limber weirdly sexy and graceful once he's been "enhanced" by the teleportation trip. It's a twitchy turn, yes, but always to an exacting purpose: the unsettling energy, mania and mood swings, and intimidating spasms of the character's sudden temper tantrums all show how the underlying transformation is beginning to accelerate; then, later, when he becomes Brundlefly, the twitching is an insectile alien body language, horrifying yet recognisable. There's a marvellous unpredictability to Goldblum in the role, from his unexpected line readings to seemingly improvised beats, my favourite being when he storms out of the apartment after a row with Veronica, then completely out of nowhere, leaps up to tap the hanging light fitting as he sweeps away along the hallway. It's an absolutely physical performance, which is taken to the next level as the mutation peaks, hobbling pathetically with the aid of walking sticks, hunched and malevolent, or scuttling across walls and ceiling (an effect achieved, pre-CGI, with the whole ceiling set being built into a huge Ferris wheel which is rotated to create the illusion of someone able to stick to walls)!

Above all, this is an intensely human portrait, even as that humanity diminishes. When Brundle hugs Veronica after she first sees him afflicted by those horrific changes, and his ear falls off, his abject terror is heartbreaking and raw.

Geena Davis as the other half of the central doomed duo, science journalist Veronica, does excellent work as well, complementing Goldblum's febrile intensity. Their initial scenes of sparring flirtation go down so well, it makes otherwise clunky exposition sing. Later, as the story darkens, she poignantly reveals the emotional toll of their disintegrating relationship, a potent analogue for watching someone ravaged by a terrible disease yet being powerless to help. But Veronica is steely too, no limp whimpering screamer, delivering the film's infamous tag-line with an ominous snap. It's one of the significant achievements of the film that Cronenberg manages to capture a real-life couple who also have great chemistry on-screen! I'm very partial to the work of oft overlooked John Getz as Stathis Borans (Stathis, such a Cronenbergian name!), as Veronica's slimy, smirking editor and stalkery ex. He's just such colossal dick...And yet, by the end, weirdly sympathetic as well. It's another finely layered turn. *The Fly* soars as much due to its performances as its splatter!

Ultimately, though, the quality which links *The Fly* back to those unsettling kids TV shows of my childhood is its underlying oddness. This is no simple slasher flick nor one-track gorefest. It's gnarly and peculiar and alluringly strange. It boasts wild surreal images such as the classic abortion/maggot birthing scene (complete with witty little cameo from Cronenberg himself as the masked surgeon), but also literary references – Kafka's *Metamorphosis*, "I'm an insect who dreamt he was a man" – and Brundle's unforgettable speech about "insect politicians" which stems from Cronenberg's own time as an entomologist and his fascination with insect societies, which are both recognisibly structured like human populations, yet utterly alien.

Another quality which adds to this idiosyncratic tone is Cronenberg's bone-dry sense of humour. *The Fly* is packed with pitch-black gags and joyfully deadpan comic beats. Brundle telling his detached body parts, "You're relics, yes you are," and joking that his bathroom cabinet where he stores them is the Brundle Museum of Natural History, or that the "Life and Times of Brundlefly" would make a great picture book for kids (before demonstrating how he eats by liquefying the food with acid vomit)!

One anecdote from the director's commentary seems to crystallise this singular voice. When recording Howard Shore's score, producer Mel Brooks (yes, that Mel Brooks – which makes it even odder, right?) asked whether the music was too extreme at certain places. He noted one specific moment where the score crescendos as Brundle moves along the sidewalk. "The guy is just walking down the street," Brooks accused. "No, Mel," replied Cronenberg, "The guy is about to meet his destiny."

When you dig down, *The Fly* is just extra, well, weird.

The film's ultimate genius, however, is its humanity, and how it weaponises that aspect against the audience. The concept of metamorphosis is incredibly potent. It can be both empowering and horrific, but Cronenberg explicitly uses it to mirror the processes of illness and ageing. *The Fly* confronts us with our own mortality in the most graphic fashion. Cronenberg has described in interviews how *The Fly* is the story of two lovers, one of whom contracts a terminal illness, and that their partner is then forced to witness their decline, before ultimately helping them to commit suicide. It's a far too bleak and unsparing scenario to play as straight drama, but abstracting it into science fiction horror really allows Cronenberg retain that central gut-punch while also extending these ideas to imaginatively ghoulish extremes. He offers: "But you have to consider how many people have given themselves their own death sentence in their bathrooms by discovering that thing in the shower or in the bathtub or in the mirror. That's where the potency of those scenes comes from."

It is why our dying protagonist spends so much time looking into the bathroom mirror and meticulously archiving his dissolution, why Brundle remains so eloquent throughout the film, whereas in the original 1950s version the scientist is left mute during the closing act. Brundle is narrating his disease, something Cronenberg found very "enlightening" in first person accounts of terminal patients he read in preparation for the script. They explained in their own words from the inside what they were going through.

This is why the characters are so relatable. Why it's crucial the performances are so human and sympathetic. This is at the heart of body horror's power and dreadful appeal: its relatability. Brundle even references it in passing: "Society's grey fear of the flesh." Body horror is the ultimate universal genre. We want to look away, but we can't. We're all staring into the mirror every day of our lives, witnessing the inevitable, the inexorable. It's the same thing I was so unsettled by in those *Doctor Who* half-creatures long ago. *The Fly* makes it clear we are all those half-creatures, or will one day become them. Whether we begin as horror fans or become them later on, we will all become the horror in the end.

That's truly terrifying.

Be afraid, be very afraid.

THE BIRDS

BY

HARRY MANFREDINI

Composer

Friday the 13th Parts 1-10, Wishmaster, Swamp Thing, House 1-4, DeepStar Six, The Hills Have Eyes II

HarryManfredini.com

Let me explain. You might expect my choice to be *Friday the 13th* just from a monetary standpoint. Or maybe *The Exorcist*, which many think of as the best horror film. But no. I choose *The Birds* for one reason only. This is the most terrifying film I've ever seen. Even when I watched it again after many years in order to write this article, I still flinched, which will be explained shortly. Another thing that might surprise you, since I am a film composer, is that I chose a film with NO SCORE. I will explain this as well.

I have a strange fear of birds, especially when they are flying around inside a house. It comes from my older sister, who was 18 when I was born. I was just a small child, and she would just freak out when my mother would let her pet bird out of the cage. I guess by osmosis I felt the fear and incorporated it into my psyche. Even to this day, I am not completely bird-terror-free.

Let's get to the film...

The Birds was released in 1963, directed and produced by Alfred Hitchcock after his classic *Psycho. The Birds* stars Tippi Hedren, Rod Taylor, Jessica Tandy, and Suzanne Pleshette, based on a short story by Daphne du Maurier.

If you, the reader, have not seen this film (which is very possible), you might want to check it out before continuing... but it is not necessary.

I can tell you that many consider this film to be Hitchcock at his best, and maybe even his best film. There are others who find it to be awful, and yes, maybe his worst. Think Ed Wood. I will let you find out for yourself which club you fit in. I think it is at least genius for many reasons, but I warn that others feel the opposite for possibly the same reasons.

The score. Film fans, of course, connect the great Bernard Herrmann with Hitchcock Films. *The Birds* has no score. Herrmann recorded some bird sounds, fluttering, screeching and such. Remi Gassmann and Oskar Sala are credited with using these sounds to give an aural sense to the visuals. But for sure, NO MUSIC. As a film composer, I can tell you that any score, no matter who composed it, would ruin this film. As any composer will tell you, silence is a huge part of any score. Where there is music or where there is no music is very critical to the dramatic effect of any film. In this film, the silence is terrifying. In a scored film, you are often not even aware of the music. In this film you are on the edge of your seat because of the silence.

Many young film fans may find the pace and plot to be very slow and frustrating, but once the terror starts, it is relentless - well worth the wait even if it's halfway through the 119 minutes!

Hitchcock's brilliance with a camera is evident in so many scenes. I will touch on a few shortly. The main characters are solid and strange as their personalities and arcs become revealed to us. There are also numerous minor characters who both add to the tension and also offer a nice touch of comic relief.

The film begins as a light romantic comedy. Rod Taylor as Mitch Brenner, a handsome and successful lawyer, enters a pet store to buy some love birds for his niece. Hedren plays Melanie Daniels, a rich socialite who is looking for love and something of value in her life and is attracted to Mitch. She poses as the owner of the store (who is in the back room) and keeps his interest for a while. But when a bird escapes from her grasp, he realizes she is not the bird lady in charge. She finds out enough about him to know he lives in Bodega Bay with his mother and niece. Not giving up on her quest for the strapping Mitch, she buys two love birds and drives up to surprise him and his niece in a mysterious way. She learns of his location from a town local, and information about the niece from a school teacher, Suzanne Pleshette, who we also learn was Mitch's ex-girlfriend. Melanie rents a boat, crosses the bay and surreptitiously places the birds in the house and makes her escape, only to get noticed by Mitch, who is a bit intrigued. As she returns the boat, a seagull quickly attacks on her, foreshadowing what's to come.

Melanie manages to stay the weekend by renting a room in the home of the ex-girlfriend.

As Melanie and the teacher talk, we learn about Mitch. His father died, and his mom is very traumatized by the loss. Mom is both strange and very protective of Mitch, played to a tee by Jessica Tandy. As the story slowly moves forward, the birds, for unknown and unexplained reasons, attack...and once this avian evil starts, the film does not let up. The ending remains as unanswered as is the reason for the sudden attacks. Many minor characters offer theories for the terror, including the usual "end of the world" drunk bible thumper and a woman who says it is Melanie's fault, that she is evil and brought it to the town. Even a bird authority pitches in with theories as well. Most of this takes place in The Tides restaurant/diner/bar in town. To me, the reason for the attacks really does not matter, because it's just happening and it's not good; an unexplained disaster of biblical proportions. Any explanation will fall short and not be very comforting anyway.

The rather simple plot becomes more interesting as we learn of the main characters. Melanie is without a mother; Mitch has no father. The mom is so spooky you might think of a Mrs. Bates before she was stuffed! Melanie even arcs from rich-bitch to a bit of a mother to the young niece. The characters are solid, not just cardboard cutouts.

We should also remember the effects are practical, and some are astounding. No CGI here - it's a 1963 film. At times, you may be wondering, "How the hell did they do that?"

Probably the scene most often cited is where Melanie sits outside the school and lights a cigarette while the children sing an old folk song titled "Ristle-tee, Rossle-tee," a strange song that seems to go on forever. At this point, we the audience have already been treated to a couple of bird attacks. As Melanie sits, we see a black crow or two land on the monkey bars in the playground behind her. Cut back to Melanie as she puffs. The next shot reveals a few more birds, then another cut, and then more. The tension rises for the audience as Melanie is totally oblivious to what is going on. In the final shot, literally hundreds of huge black crows are waiting to attack. Melanie suddenly becomes aware, so she rushes into the school to try to rescue the children. As they run out to what seems like safety, the birds attack...and it gets pretty intense.

Another scene has Melanie stuck in a phone booth with birds smashing and cracking the glass, like she is the one in the cage and helpless, recalling the iconic shower scene in *Psycho*.

Speaking of *Psycho*, later in the movie, Melanie goes up to the attic to check out damage, only to find the birds have broken through the roof. As she enters and the door closes, they attack. She tries to escape. If you think the *Psycho* shower scene was intense, this blows it out of the water.

There is another scene where hundreds of birds simply fly out of the open fireplace into the living room, raging and wreaking havoc on our little family of mom, lawyer, niece and Melanie.

I get flustered by just one bird flying around in a room, this was completely traumatic for me!!

Hitchcock's camera bends and moves with amazing angles and framing to tell so much of the story, from a "bird's eye" view of the town (pun intended) to the cute little love birds swaying as Melanie drives through the turns on her way to Bodega Bay.

Rather interesting scenes take place in The Tides Restaurant, where multiple, interwoven dialogue sections prove to be Altman-esque before Altman-esque was a thing. The unexplained and uneventful ending with no real finality even evokes some future Romero.

Those who hate this film rant about the slow, dumb plot, the silly birds and effects, and, of course, the unexplained reasons for it even happening. They find the actors weak and dull. They see all the "art" of film as simply the art hanging out for its own reason. Some say it is *MST3K* material.

I suppose they could really have some fun of this film, but I think *MST3K* could do a pretty good job with any horror film. It's not that hard to do.

My one criticism of the film is the opening credits, with the shadows and birds flying around. It gave away too much as to what would follow, but that's just me.

It is true that the effects, by today's standards, are pretty old hat and the dialogue is a bit dated, but we're dealing with 1963 here. In my opinion, this movie remains as fresh and maybe even more interesting than many of today's horror films.

Watch it, or revisit it, and decide for yourself.

Some interesting trivia: Tippi Hedren's daughter is Melanie Griffith, who is named after the character in the film.

SESSION 9

BY

PAULA LINDBERG

Actor/Producer

American Mary, Supernatural, Fringe,
A Tale of Two Coreys, Blood Bus

Instagram: @PaulaALindberg Twitter: @PaulaLindberg

PaulaLindberg.com

Session 9 is a criminally underrated gem that scares the hell out of me. Sometimes our favorite movies are not our favorites because they are the most critically acclaimed thing we've ever seen, but more so that they found us at just the right time.

As an actor, I've always been driven to explore characters completely outside of myself. The thin line between sanity and insanity has always fascinated me; what pushes someone over that line? How can seemingly normal people do unspeakable acts? Those themes, plus a penchant for outdated & torturous medical procedures (bloodletting & lobotomies anyone?), and an obsession with architecture and buildings in a state of decay makes *Session 9* the whole package for me.

Part of the reason this film resonated with me was that I watched it shortly after a trip to my favorite used bookstore in Victoria, BC. It was there I found a book that I still think about to this day called *The Summer of the Black Sun*, by Bill T. O'Brien. The author had apparently spent time in a mental institution, then went to university, wrote one book, and died. The book itself is about an ostensibly normal person who gradually ends up institutionalized and lobotomized but every step of the way, you think, "OMG, that could be me. I could make those missteps." And it's horrifying.

Around that time, I also had a relative and childhood playmate diagnosed as schizophrenic. It was so difficult to see how fragile we are to these small glitches in our brains. How a chemical imbalance can make real-life horrors actually exist in front of you. Isn't that what we're mostly afraid of: losing control of ourselves? *Session 9* capitalizes on these themes and then elevates with a possible possession angle; something I will never admit I'm terrified of, because ghosts are not real! (Right? Right???)

We try to look at people with mental illness as 'the other,' someone who is not like us, or could never be us, and this book tore down those walls. It forged a path for me as an actor, where I try to approach characters without judgment. You get to go down a path that is totally foreign, and you can see yourself making those decisions as the character; the exhilarating challenge of resolving issues in situations so far removed from your own life.

It reminds me of the first time I fell in love with acting. I was in grade eight and painfully shy, yet I got cast in the school play as a gang member who murdered someone in a gang fight. It was so revelatory that I could play someone who was so different from me, someone who didn't suffer the crippling social anxiety that I normally experienced. It was empowering. That's where I first felt like an actor and – to this day – it's what fuels my creative process.

For those of you who missed it, *Session 9* follows an asbestos removal crew charged with cleaning out an abandoned insane asylum. In the course of their work in this isolated building, the audiotapes of a past patient with multiple personalities are discovered and tensions arise between the co-workers with disastrous – and fatal – results.

I love that the pacing is deliberate and takes its time during the film's first half, a device reminiscent of personal favorites like Tobe Hooper's claustrophobic *The Texas Chain Saw Massacre* and Ridley Scott's slow-burning *Alien*. It's brooding and smoldery; like a meditation inside someone else's brain, full of hints and symbols. So many movies rely on jump scares, that allowing for a slow build gives us the creepy, get-under-your-skin kind of movie. Atmospheric, subtle; you can't watch it just once. And the score is creepy and blood-chillingly simple. The scene where Brandon Sexton III runs past all those suits lined up in the tunnel with the giant rubber gloves reaching for him...genius. Yes, you do have to watch David Curuso act, but Brandon Sexton III with a mullet? Totally worth it.

Session 9 explores themes like paranoia and isolation similar to a couple of my other favorite movies. *John Carpenter's The Thing* has Macready's men trapped by terror within the elements, their strengths and weaknesses fully exposed. Can you trust those around you? Can you trust yourself? Who's done what? And when? The tension in *Session 9* slowly builds because – also like Stanley Kubrick's *The Shining* (a movie my mother accidentally let me watch at age 7) – events are filtered through the prism of an unreliable narrator. Can we trust what we see? Is our protagonist actually mentally ill (or possessed)? Also, we're constantly asking; is it possession, cabin fever, or something even more sinister?

Almost the entire movie is shot in Danvers State Hospital (aka the State Lunatic Hospital at Danvers), which is itself a character in the film. Opened in 1878, how amazing it is that we have all this footage of it before it got torn down just five years later. The slow-burning fear that exists in every shot, from the peeling paint to the creepy murals, the hospital lends this unsettling quality that plays like another character lurking in every frame. I love how the director makes use of the underground tunnels connecting the buildings. In the 1930s and '40s, the hospital was so overcrowded, apparently patients were forced to sleep down there. You can't help but think of all the horrific stories that those walls contain. And as much as I don't really believe in ghosts (no, really!), just imagine if those walls could talk! What macabre stories they must tell. The anguish and the torment. I remember reading that actor Peter Mullan also reported strange happenings on the set. He said, while filming on the roof, there was a voice in his head telling him to jump off 'to see what would happen.' He said the building brought out a morbid kind of 'overactive curiosity.' The filmmakers apparently used real items from the hospital as set dressing – like old patient tissue and blood samples - some of which they refused to film out of fear.

It's a fear that I understand. In Vancouver, every actor at some point shoots at Riverside Hospital. It's an old abandoned mental hospital that, while supercool and creepy, is really the poor man's Danvers. Terrifying stories of its history abound and I would never allow myself to be alone there. One day, I was sitting in my cast chair that was set up in the old bath area, and was sitting with at least 6 other people when, all of a sudden, I glanced up and I was completely alone. There was no way 6 people could have noiselessly removed themselves from the room. One of our AD's actually quit because all the doors – which she had previously propped open – all suddenly slammed shut at the same time. We actually had production shut down one day when a 'resident' escaped. Big old haunted buildings. Love 'em…and hate 'em.

Session 9 takes you on a deep and dark journey into the human psyche, which is exactly where I want to go as an actor to explore character...like a forced vacation inside someone else's fucked up brain. But mercifully, it's only for two hours.

THE LEOPARD MAN

BY

PAUL HAYNES

Writer/Producer

I'll Be Gone in the Dark (Series), *DVD Beaver*, *The Indie*,
I'll Be Gone in the Dark (Book), *Los Angeles Magazine*
Twitter/Instagram: @ThePaulOfHaynes

The primary challenge in writing about my favorite horror movie for this volume is choosing just one. There are many I value greatly, and it's tempting to break the rules and write about multiple - perhaps, at least in part, for the self-serving purpose of flaunting the breadth of my taste. But now that I've confessed that, I feel a duty to discipline and good taste to avoid naming any of the ones that didn't make the cut.

Then again, fuck good taste. What could be more antithetical to the spirit of cinema's most ill-reputed genre? Besides, I've already piqued the curiosity of you, the reader, who could reasonably argue it's now my moral burden to satisfy it. So then, know that *Don't Look Now* (1973), *The Wicker Man* (1973), *The Shining* (1980), *Freaks* (1932), Cronenberg's remake of *The Fly* (1986), *Rosemary's Baby* (1968), and Bob Clark's one-two punch of *Deathdream* (1974) and *Black Christmas* (1974) all vie competitively for first place. And if you consider it a proper horror film, Michael Powell's devastatingly perfect, and perfectly devastating, *Peeping Tom* (1960) towers formidably over everything.

But what exactly is a horror film? Answering that question is not unlike trying to define love. You know it when you encounter it, but an absolute definition is elusive. What generically distinguishes horror from mystery from thriller from fantasy? Is *Jaws* a horror movie or an adventure film? Is *Alien* a creature feature or science fiction? Is *The Silence of the Lambs* properly a thriller or a slasher? Likewise *Psycho*, whose occasional classification as a horror movie always feels wrong to me. And I still struggle to categorize *Paperhouse*, which I'd long remembered as an *Elm Street*-esque supernatural shocker until a refresher viewing revealed something closer to a postmodernist young-adult gothic fantasy. While it may seem that horror boasts a streamlined canon, some of its most venerated works challenge that notion.

Putting the genre-busters aside however, a bona fide horror film and its generic conventions really aren't hard to spot. The usual requisites of commercial feature films—character development, careful narrative construction, logical consistency, etc.—are often, if not entirely absent, secondary to, and wholly at the service of the business of crafting a nightmare. And like a true nightmare, fear and dread are the engines of the horror film. At their worst, horror films can be crude and exploitative, mindlessly reveling in sadism. It's an unfortunate reality of this genre that most entries slum near the bottom rung. But at their best, horror films implement all the sensory and aesthetic tools of the cinema - in a way that no other medium can - conjure fear, dread, and impending doom. It is one of the few mainstream genres, alongside sketch comedy and animation, in which the avant-garde can exist without controversy. Horror is arguably the most cinematic of genres.

For me, the soul of the horror film is the fear of the dark, of the unknown, of what the eye cannot quite register. It's the dread of what creeps in the blank spots out of view; of that which hides in the shadows. And *The Leopard Man* (1943) is a film rapturously draped in shadows. Shadows that ooze like black honey from and back into unseen reservoirs, coiling around the film like a patiently lethal constrictor. Shadows that linger in the foreground of shot after shot, underscoring the inescapable fate that awaits the victim walking into them—or rather, being sucked into them, like terrestrial black holes of bad fortune. The shadows bleed into the film's thematic repertoire, whereby a boy's ominous shadow puppets both foretell and later call back to a character's savage death; the shadow of a window washer's squeegee descends upon the somber proceedings at a funeral parlor, augmenting the sense of business happening and life moving on in the wake of death. Shadows are the movie's connective tissue. Shadows are its soul.

The Leopard Man is the third and least celebrated of a cycle of three horror pictures Jacques Tourneur directed for producer Val Lewton. The first two were *Cat People* (1941)—the most esteemed among a quite impressive slate of horror films Lewton produced at RKO—and *I Walked with a Zombie*, released two weeks before *The Leopard Man*. *Cat People* aside, Tourneur is best known for *Out of the Past*, the sinuous 1947 crime thriller starring Robert Mitchum and Kirk Douglas that often tops lists of great film noir. But Tourneur, a second-generation director (he was the son of French émigré Maurice Tourneur, who worked mainly in the silent era), is often overlooked in the pantheon of Golden Age auteurs.

My formal introduction to Tourneur's body of work was at New York's Walter Reade Theater in 2002, where a major retrospective (reprised in 2018) programmed by the Film Society of Lincoln Center showcased Tourneur's versatility across a filmography that spanned horror, sci-fi, westerns, crime pictures, spy thrillers, jungle adventures, swashbucklers, and melodrama. Tourneur was a great and prolific genre director with a poet's soul, and few films exemplify this better than the unjustly forgotten 1950 western *Stars in My Crown*, a heartrending memory piece of bittersweet nostalgia shot through with an arrow of brutal truth, probing the dark colonialist (and segregationist) spirit of the American frontier.

Darkness abounds throughout Tourneur's work, and none is blacker than *The Leopard Man*. Clocking in at a lean 66 minutes, what it lacks in the layered psychosexual undertow of *Cat People* and moody lyricism of *I Walked with a Zombie*, it makes up for in pure heart-stopping terror. Narrative-wise, it's almost elementary in its simplicity: in an economically depressed New Mexico bordertown, a black leopard is borrowed by a showgirl to one-up her competitor, but her castanet-wielding rival intentionally spooks the cat, and the animal breaks free and flees into the night. Soon after, women in town begin turning up dead and mutilated. Though the leopard is initially presumed responsible, debate slowly swells over whether the killings might be the work of some unknown man "with a kink in his brain."

About seven minutes in begins what may be the scariest movie sequence ever filmed. A teenage girl is hectored by her Mamacita into walking across town late at night to replenish the family's cornmeal supply for their tortillas, lest rumors circulate that the family can't afford to buy food. Despite the girl's protests, her Mamacita shoves her out the door and locks it behind her, forbidding her back inside until she has fetched the cornmeal.

The girl steps out into the night air and immediately a chill comes over her. She just misses closing time at the nearby grocery store and is turned away by an owner unwilling to be inconvenienced. The only alternative is the market on the far edge of town, and the next shot—a wide angle on a lonely railroad bridge, cutting across a dimly moonlit arroyo in the desert expanse, as the girl walks tentatively toward its pitch-black underpass—is one that plays on multiple fundamental fears simultaneously. Claustrophobia, agoraphobia, and fear of the dark are equally stirred, which is indeed what makes the outdoors so attractive to horror pictures. Few relatable scenarios are more unsettling than being outside, alone, in the almost-still, almost-silent dark of night. But the wilderness here isn't the typical woodsy tangle; instead, it's the eerily pale Southwestern landscape where lurking danger is obscured not by trees but by the inky blots of blackness where moonlight doesn't reach.

Without spoiling the pleasures of this sequence, suffice it to say that what unfolds is a master class in the use of light and shadows, quiet and loud, what happens in and out of frame, to invoke terror at its most primal and distilled.

The Leopard Man was shot quickly and cheaply, but not without care. In fact, its threadbareness is a virtue, without tradition-de-qualité pretensions or compulsory narrative padding diluting its impact. Tourneur packs heaps of subtle visual poetry and thematic richness into a sharply efficient narrative that yields what could be considered a proto-proto-slasher—but without sacrificing a core humanity. The loss of each victim is deeply felt, and the grief of their loved ones hangs somberly over the film. And, more significantly—and revealing the film's noir adjacence—so does guilt. Poor Mamacita, whose hardhearted authoritarianism cost her daughter her life, shows up again midway through the movie, crossing herself at her doorway while intoning "Válgame dios"—God help me. And the cemetery caretaker who locks up the grounds when he should know full well there's a girl about to be trapped inside its walls. In all of the film's deaths, characters who are clearly not the killer are nevertheless either partly responsible or feel compelled to shoulder responsibility. Most of the police chief's dialogue consists of him absolving people of blame.

Adapted from *Black Alibi* (1942) by Cornell Woolrich—one of the most screen-adapted of novelists, whose works became films by directors as diverse as Truffaut, Fassbinder, and Hitchcock (namely, *Rear Window*)—*The Leopard Man* milks its setting without quite exoticizing it. In fact, the economic reality of this sleepy desert resort town is drawn with a despairing clarity. The undercurrent of financial hardship runs through every scene, and issues around money are key to setting in motion the events that lead to each victim's untimely demise. Class is fate. Meanwhile, stark social disparity is addressed with lightheartedly satiric derision when a wealthy Chicana is awakened on the morning of her birthday by her attendants gently serenading her.

This is one of only a handful of scenes that take place in the daylight hours. *The Leopard Man* is a nocturnal beast steeped in that particular creeping panic that rolls in like a slow tide as the reassuring sounds of civilization fade into the distance. It is a movie of the night, through and through—and fundamentally noir—that has a keen feel for the seductive fragmentation of objects and events after dark.

The clittering of the castanets. A pair of high-heeled legs illuminated briefly by a flashlight beam before the street returns to black. The fortune teller's disembodied arm jutting out of a window, beckoning with a hand of cards. The quiet sense of dread as night descends on a cemetery. The eeriness of the dusty night wind. A tumbleweed's false alarm. The silent, gazing marble face above a gravestone. The pointy peaks crowning an assembly of hooded figures against a cloudy night sky. It's a procession of images and moments (including a literal procession) that, even more upon reflection, assumes the haunting disconnectedness of a dream.

But *The Leopard Man*, while stylistically dreamlike, is also doggedly fatalistic. The image that bookends the film—a ball in perpetual levitation on the crest of a fountain jet—announces this clearly. The inevitability of some predetermined fate, leaving us at the mercy of forces beyond our grasp; the soul-staining weight of guilt on those who, for now, escape that fate—it all comes with the territory of noir. And the sum of dreams, fatalism, and guilt is nightmares.

The Leopard Man, in its black pearl elegance, is a sweetly beautiful nightmare.

EVIL DEAD II

BY

MIKE MENDEZ

Filmmaker

Big Ass Spider, The Gravedancers, Tales of Halloween

Twitter/Instagram: @MadmanMendez

There's the best movie and there's your favorite movie. Often they are not the same. If we are talking about things like structure, cinematography, acting, and directing, I would probably point you over to William Friedkin's *The Exorcist*, which I still find to be one of the most terrifying and dread-inducing movies ever made. But we are talking about my favorite horror movie and that is a very different thing. You can throw out the structure and the form...and you can be radical. You can be revolutionary; you can ignore the rules and change the game forever.

So, with that in mind, my favorite horror movie is Sam Raimi's 1987 demon classic *Evil Dead II*. This movie is more than just a film to me. It was my film school. In my formative high school years, this was the movie I turned to when I wanted to learn about the art of filmmaking. Through Sam Raimi's innovative and wild use of camera movement, it broke down the walls of classic filmmaking and presented a radical alternative brimming with imagination and maniacal glee.

Everything from stop motion, puppetry, miniatures, and hundreds of gallons of fake blood were used to bring this story to life. The story was simple: a guy stuck in a cabin must fend off the forces of evil. Even that simple storyline defies conventional filmmaking. This movie shouldn't work. There's nothing to it. It's a very simple premise, yet this film is not dull for a second and delights from start to finish as a carnal feast for the senses.

Bruce Campbell plays his signature role of "Ash" in this sequel/quasi-remake of *Evil Dead*. Even that defies convention. It's not even a real sequel. The first 15 minutes are basically a slight retelling of the first movie and then it goes off from there. There's even a splice point where you could cut the two movies together and it would make perfect sense. If you cut right from the last frame of *Evil Dead* right to the stop motion sequence of Ash flying and you'd have one continuous 3 hour film, truly making it the ultimate experience in grueling terror.

The first time I saw it was when it came out in the theater. I was 14 years old and it was playing at one of my local theaters in Glendale, California. I saw it on a matinee because that's what my family did. I wish I could say it was a revelatory moment where I had a near religious experience and my life changed forever, but sadly this was not the case. I don't think I was ready for it. I was used to the classic structure of horror films. At that time, I would've expected a slasher film or something.

But it didn't give me that. It gave me something different and, at first, I thought something was wrong with the film. I was dead wrong - something was wrong with me. My little 14-year-old brain had not developed enough to appreciate a movie that thought and was conceived totally out of the box. I left the theater snickering, "That was laughable," and it was - intentionally laughable. I was just too stupid to understand that.

But you can't keep a genius film like this down. It wouldn't be long before it reared its demonic head at me again and snarled, "Join us." I believe I came across it again on VHS, and then again and again on cable. Then I got it. I was hooked. I wanted to read every article I could about it. I wanted to share it with everyone I knew (and I did).

Back then, much like now, I hung out with a group of movie-loving geeks, so *Evil Dead II* stuck with them like white on rice. At that time, we were making little shorts with our parents' video cameras in our backyard. Pretty soon, *Evil Dead II* had infected our brains the way the evil infected Ash's hand. Bloody horror comedies were all I was interested in making. My director of photography and one of my best friends, Rod, was interested in how to move the camera that way. How do we make our own shaky cam? Wheelchairs and shopping carts were acquired. Rear screen projection was implemented and gallons and gallons of fake blood was concocted in my kitchen, much to the chagrin of my mother. It only evolved from there. Pretty soon, I was learning how to do face casts. Foam latex would be baking in my oven, and all my hard-earned money from my weekend jobs was poured into making our silly movies. We were making them more for ourselves than an actual audience. I went to an All-Boys Catholic School, so what's a nerdy teenager to do other than makeup your friends and spray copious amounts of fake blood on everything.

In the truest sense, *Evil Dead II* was our film school. It's where we learned about lenses, camera movement, backwards photography, stop motion FX, and editing, particularly through stylized montages. The list goes on and on. I'm sure I watched the film several hundred times over those formative years. Just to make it more exciting, when reading *Fangoria Magazine* and *Cinefantastique*, we learned that Sam Raimi was back at it, and a third part in the series was coming, originally entitled *The Medieval Dead*, a title I actually prefer to *Army of Darkness*. That's a whole other obsession and I could probably write several essays on how important that film was to me as well.

But it all started for me with *Evil Dead II*. There are scarier films, there are more thought-provoking films, but *Evil Dead II* hit me in a way that no other movie had at that point. It inspired me as a filmmaker. The inventive "can do" attitude of that film, the genre blending, and the breakneck pace of that film inspired me in a way no film had before. Without any hyperbole, I honestly believe I wouldn't be making films today if three kids from Michigan hadn't inspired me with their crazy, fevered dreams about a book bound in human flesh in a spooky cabin in the woods. I still hold that there is a fingerprint that can be traced back to *Evil Dead II* in everything I've ever made, and it's a tradition I don't think is ever going to stop.

THE HUNGER

BY

EDWARD W. STEPHENS III

Film Festival Co-Founder/Writer/Graphic Artist/
Film Historian/Musical Cacophonist

Zed Fest Film Festival

Twitter: @ZedFestFilmFest Facebook: @ZedFest

ZedFest.org

As a young man establishing my own identity in the 1980s, I was very creative in most of the arts: filmmaking, photography, graphics, music, etc., and considered myself "alternative/progressive." By night, I went out on the town in black sneakers, black jeans, a black T-shirt, and a long black trench coat. The guys and I would haunt underground nightclubs with names like Houdini's, The Shelter, and Liedernacht, dancing to new wave, alternative, and punk rock. By day, I dressed for work in black sneakers, black jeans, a black T-Shirt, and black sport gloves as a key grip on Detroit-area film productions, filming industrial films with cars, robots, and talking heads, pushing dollies, swinging cranes, and pulling cable...but what I really wanted to do was direct.

Anyone working in the movies can attest that work in this business is generally not 9 to 5 and five days a week. It's usually two to four days of alternating, grueling labor and mind-numbing boredom…"Hurry up and wait." It was rarely steady, often with a week or two or more between gigs. So when I was not on set, I would revert to my natural state of existence as a vampire...up all night, usually penning screenplays, diving under the covers at the first sign of sunlight, not coming out of my crypt until after the sun had set.

As a kid, I loved vampire movies, and I'd go around saying, "Blah, blah, I vant to bite you in-da-neck." Throughout my life, I must have owned at least a hundred sets of those cheap plastic fangs that make you drool all over yourself. My go-to Halloween costume was invariably Dracula...except when my mom became obsessed with the soap opera *Dark Shadows*, then she augmented my costume to be Barnabas Collins.

Music was always important to me. From an early age, my parents exposed me to the classics...classical orchestral/symphonic, classic rock and roll, classic rhythm and blues. At two years old I wanted to be "Bingo Tar" (Ringo Star). I started guitar lessons at 9 years old, discovered *Switched-On Bach* at 12... so when this new wave/alternative stuff came out in the '80s, I was all up for it. Orchestral Manoeuvres In The Dark's *Dazzle Ships* and especially "Close To The Edit" by The Art of Noise, opened me up to a world of musical cacophony.

You wouldn't be surprised if I confessed that my all-time favorite movie is *Blade Runner* (1982). While Ridley Scott's cosmic horror offering, *Alien* (1979) is by far one of the truly fantastic monster movies, I would have to give credit for my favorite horror movie to Ridley's brother Tony Scott and his 1983 masterpiece *The Hunger*. When you open an art film about contemporary vampires with Peter Murphy in a cage in an underground nightclub looking like the undead and singing about Bela Lugosi...well, you've got my full attention.

The Hunger, based on the novel written by Whitley Strieber (who also wrote the novels Communion and Wolfen), is a story about Miriam Blaylock, a beautiful 2,000-year-old vampire (Catherine Deneuve). Her 200-year-old lover John (David Bowie) is suddenly and quickly deteriorating with age. He seeks out a famous doctor of aging research, Dr. Sarah Roberts (Susan Sarandon) who does not believe his claim of rapid aging. The doctor decides to investigate John's claim but, upon visiting his home, Meriam tells her that John is not there anymore as she sets her sights on his replacement...Sarah.

In its time, *The Hunger* was derided as being "all style and no substance," while some hail it for opening the door to the modern Goth movement. For me, the substance was in the subtext, underlying the style. It opened doors, granting permission to express style in alternative ways, not just the styles of wardrobe, the stylish hip sunglasses that everyone wore (I've had a few pairs of *The Hunger*-like hip sunglasses myself), and not just beautiful visuals that are often described as "every individual frame is a work of art." Style, for me, was the interweaving of quality music and interesting sounds with dynamic images, cutting, pace of scene, and subtle manipulation of time.

The best example of *The Hunger*'s interweaving music and sounds while manipulating time can be found on YouTube by searching for "*The Hunger* Opening Credits". Starting in a smoke-filled nightclub, Peter Murphy singing "Bela Lugosi's Dead", intercutting with people dancing in the club, intercutting with Miriam and John making contact with a swinging couple, intercutting sound and visuals of what will happen in the near future as a car drives over a bridge, back and forth between the nightclub and the car, until the cuts of the club are images of the past and the scenario inside the car becomes the present. Not presented in the YouTube offering, the time jumping intercutting flashes to another future/present/past intermingling of a laboratory monkey inflicting deadly violence on another monkey while Miriam and John kill their swinging prey, dispose of their bodies, and Dr. Sarah Roberts laments the death of the other monkey. (Now that's how you introduce an audience to your story!)

The juxtaposition of musical styles was inspirational to me. Hearing Bauhaus one moment, Franz Schubert's "Trio in E Flat" (the recurring theme), Iggy Pop's "Funtime" and the ineffable Delibes' *Lakme*. And lest we forget Michel Rubini's chilling original atmospheric scores.

I don't know if anyone else but me ever made a *Blade Runner*/*The Hunger* "Methuselah" connection. In the July 1980 Hampton Fancher draft of the *Blade Runner* screenplay, Sebastion tells Pris that he has Methuselah Syndrome: "My glands, they grow old too fast." But in the Philip K. Dick novel *Do Androids Dream of Electric Sheep*, Sebastian did not have "Accelerated Decrepitude," he only had a bit of a low IQ and was referred to in the story as a "chickenhead." In Strieber's novel *The Hunger*, published a year later in 1981, the character Dr. Sarah Roberts is a scientist studying the effects of sleep on aging. One of her test monkeys, who is aging rapidly, is nicknamed Methuselah. In the movie version, they never mention the monkey's name and merely refer to Progeria, a genetic disorder that causes children to age quickly. No doubt that it is a coincidence, but if you think about it, you have these two brothers who are filmmakers: Ridley and Tony Scott, whose styles are considerably different, though they had a close relationship and consulted with each other frequently. Both of them released movies only ten months apart, both having rapidly aging characters and referencing Methuselah, seeking longevity, "I want more life... Father."

Methuselah is not the only connection between the two movies. Sound editor Peter Pennell worked on both *Blade Runner* and *The Hunger*, providing the somewhat cacophonous contributions. The faint clicking of Dr. Sarah Roberts' video monitor as she watches the monkey Methuselah disintegrate is reminiscent of the clicking of Rick Deckard's ESPER machine as he pans and zooms in on a 3D photograph. And again with Roberts' video machine, when it is turned off, buzzes and crackles almost exactly the way Deckard's Voight Kampff replicant detector machine does when he turns it off after interviewing Tyrell's niece Rachel. When John in *The Hunger* awakens in the waiting room of Dr. Sarah Roberts' clinic, there is a female voice on the P.A. which may actually be the same voice actor as the one on the P.A. at the beginning of Blade Runner, announcing Leon and his statistics right before his interview by blade runner Dave Holden.

As an imaginative writer myself, I now invoke "creative license" to retcon *The Hunger* into *Blade Runner.* Yes, even though *Blade Runner* came first, I have conceived of a retroactive continuity that brings a character from *The Hunger* into the *Blade Runner* universe. Commonly referred to as the "Retirement of Zohra" scene in *Blade Runner* when Rick Deckard is chasing the replicant Zohra through the street, there is an incongruous shot of a woman inside a metro cab looking straight at us. Because this shot seems so out of place in this sequence, and because the woman looks stylishly future-goth…I believe that this could actually be Dr. Sarah Roberts from *The Hunger.* Right? She is a vampire queen who can live forever, why would she not have still been alive in 2019 and moved to Los Angeles hungering for a new companion in *Blade Runner*?

On a side note: I don't smoke anymore, but upon revisiting this movie, I'm kind of surprised how much cigarette smoking there was in it and that I had been a smoker myself. Back then, I preferred Indonesian Clove cigarettes called Djarum Specials. Each of the guys I hung out with had their own preferred brands. There was not much sharing though. One guy was Dunnhills, another was into American Spirits, another preferred Egyptian tobacco, then there was the holdout...Marlboro Reds...in the box. And you were not a legitimate hipster if you did not have a real Zippo lighter. Fortunately, it was just a phase that only lasted a few years. Quitting smoking when I did had actually saved my life...just saying.

The experience of watching *The Hunger* inspired my creative writing process to fully immerse the story in music and sound. While I start with the basic idea or flavor of a story,

I build a playlist on YouTube of songs and ambient tracks to listen to while working out the treatment and writing direct references to the songs into the screenplays. (Direct reference i.e. background music, something like - "Theme from the Film of the Same Name" by Freur.)

I've got two weeks vacation coming up, enough time to revert to nocturnal mode, maybe write a new art house screenplay...*Theda-B 2095: The NoHo Vampire Android Hunter*, maybe opening with a song like "Is That All There Is?" as interpreted by Christina...

THE MONSTER SQUAD

BY

ERICK YARO WESSEL

Artist/Curator/Owner
The Mystic Museum, Bearded Lady Vintage & Oddities
Instagram: @erickyaro
@themysticmuseum @beardedladyvintage

The Monster Squad...where do I start? There are plenty of places, whether it be the kid comradery, memorable quotes, or the monster creations. They all fit into this story somewhere, but I think I'll start at the beginning. Being a fan of *Monster Squad* is due to first seeing *Stand by Me*. That movie laid the groundwork for my infinite love of the "kids in peril" genres. You know what I mean...*Goonies*, *The Gate*, *It*...*Monster Squad*! Without getting too deep into *Stand By Me* (so we can move on to what counts) it was the first movie I ever called my favorite. And to see a horror movie that captured what I saw in it blew my mind..."now that's my favorite movie".

Let me set the scene...it's Friday night, early 1988 in a small suburb outside Los Angeles. Popcorn and soda sat on the coffee table along with one random box of candy. I remember being excited. It was definitely movie night (we were only allowed to have soda on movie night). Two semi clear clamshell cases, too scratched up to see the movie titles hold these mysterious films. I wasn't at the rental shop this time around to make the pick. I stared at the VHS cases that were crookedly stacked on top of each other. One was for the family to watch and the other was for the adults later. I wasn't too concerned with that one. "What was the family pick? "Who picked it?" Ok it's time, with my sisters and brother and I now in our favorite spots, soda and popcorn in hand, the movie was revealed. *The Monster Squad.*

"What the fuck!" I said, in my head.

Don't get me wrong, you had me at *Monster*, but I had just never heard of it. How had I never heard of this before? When the words "monster" and "squad " come together this is something I should be aware of. With a name I already loved, we killed the light and pressed play. I mean we had to actually press play. Someone had to get up and walk to the TV and press a button. It was 1988.

This movie had it all. Everything that resonated with me at least. A group of kids fighting monsters. But not just any monsters, the most famous of monsters. I instantly felt like one of them. It was easy to relate with the characters. Not only was I similar in their age, but I was kinda a dork who loved monsters. Riding BMX bikes, building club houses, and getting bullied, I was definitely in the goddamn club.

I must have said, "kick him in the nards," 1000 times in the next week, then my brother actually kicked me in the nards (maybe the one downside of the movie). It became my go-to Halloween movie. I felt like I had to introduce everyone I met to this masterpiece.

Just like *G.I. Joe* or *He-Man*, good vs. bad, both had their teams, and in *The Monster Squad* it was perfectly matched. The monster designs and makeup effects nailed it and hold up. Dracula looked liked every dad's vampire Halloween costume from the '80s. You weren't mad at it because it was so recognizable for a kid. The Mummy was traditional, yet had a new element of creepy. Wolfman blended the original with a teenage werewolf vibe but somehow felt new and iconic. Frankenstein's monster was classic. Gill Man to this day is still my favorite monster design ever, an incredible reimagining of the *Creature From the Black Lagoon*.

After watching the movie, all I wanted was to have that core group of friends to ride around the streets with and raise hell. It really helped develop my life and friendships. My career choices started with trespassing in graveyards with friends. Now, an owner of an oddity shop and a museum of the occult with horror pop-ups, I keep that core friendship in mind, collecting macabre antiques with the passion of the kid who first saw *Monster Squad*. "Is this antique the amulet that will send evil back to purgatory?" My museum features real mummy artifacts and it's not a coincidence that I go ghost hunting either. It's as close to battling supernatural creatures as you can get. So go ahead give me the monster test...see if I pass.

PHOTO BY: REBA VERA - KING KONG HAND BY: KEN HALL

KING KONG (1933)

BY
ALEXIS IACONO

Actor/Producer
Laff Mobb's Laff Tracks, World of Warcraft: Legion, Nation's Fire, Xenophobia
Instagram: @Alexis_Iacono
Twitter: @ AlexisIacono Facebook: @alexis.iacono.7

"It was beauty who killed the beast."

The damsel in distress effect is a man saving the woman. Perhaps the woman wants to be saved, or just maybe, Ann Darrow saves Kong.

But let's cut to "present day," where crap sells and social media makes us afraid of experiencing "human touch." Instead, we get talentless, duck-faced, wanna-be models, rappers and, let's not forget, actresses posting selfies and hashtagging "actress," "famous," "sexy," and my favorite…"Instagram influencers."

I remember walking in the West Village of New York City, a carefree 12-year-old headed to acting classes at HB Studio on a beautiful blue-sky day. Little did I know, this particular day would season my creative path for life.

I was asked to improv for Trudy Steibl's class. Those who know me know I have no filter. I improvised a scene and apparently I chewed the scenery. After class, my coach Ms. Steibl approached me and said, "I do not believe in favoritism, but I need to speak to your parents." The next thing I knew, I was in the Chelsea apartment of director Robert Crest auditioning for the role of a young Fay Wray in her play *The Meadowlark*.

Days later, I woke up from a 12-year-old nap to my mother's gentle touch on my back with a little "wake up" shake. She said, "Alexis, you got the part."

I know I am supposed to write about my "favorite" horror movie. Truth is, I hate clowns, and I have a twisted sexual fascination with Alex from *A Clockwork Orange*. I mean, let's face it, nothing is more frightening than screaming and jiggling girls being tied up. Ha! So, I decided to write about the greatest horror love story of all: *King Kong*.

I was already familiar with Kong. My father and I loved *Mighty Joe Young* because it had a happy ending, but truth be told, as a young girl who believed in romance, there is nothing more frighteningly beautiful than Kong. I not only believe in life imitating art, I experienced it.

In *King Kong*, the most frightening scene was when they were all on the *Steam Ship Venture*, a tramp steamer, cruising into the fog of the unknown. Perhaps it was because I was experiencing my own Ann Darrow moment of 'exciting anxiety' upon entering my own fog.

In my late 20's, years after *The Meadowlark*, I constantly exchanged letters, as well as holiday/birthday phone calls, with Fay. Later, I took an identical boat heading to Molokai Island (aka Island of the Lepers) in Hawaii to walk the steps of Father Damien. I never felt so free and scared in my life. It was then I thought of Ann Darrow being swallowed up into the unknown. I too experienced that feeling because Molokai Mountain looked just like Skull Island, something I will never forget. The damp chills on my Maui sun-kissed arms were slowly melting as I heard the chilling Kong tribesman chants repeating in my mind. Many fantasize about exploring a jungle, but those who actually have know one thing. We are not in control. It is unequivocally pure survival.

It was never Kong nor the endless forest that truly frightened me, though. It was all of the obstacles interfering with what Kong was trying to express: love.

Horror for me is to be held back. Not by chained chrome steel, but from being unable to tell someone the truth, how you REALLY feel, being personally persecuted, falsely accused and trapped without a voice, or distracted by planes while atop the Empire State Building only trying to be understood, but instead falling endlessly to a long, heartbreaking silent death.

There's an interesting poetic justice in Kong falling - to his freedom and in love. As Ann Darrow runs to his lifeless body, perhaps it was she that finally freed his caged soul and saved him.

In passing conversation, comic cons, and podcast interviews, I am asked the same question: "Alexis, since you worked so closely with Fay and continued a friendship after the show, what was the one thing she taught you? And, if you had the chance today, what would be the one thing you wished you asked?"

A feeling of guilt and stupidity often crosses my overthinking mind and, truth be told, when I spent months in rehearsals with Fay, followed with a plethora of personal moments, private and professional breakfasts, lunches and dinner parties, I can honestly say, I learned nothing. It may seem like a slap in Fay's face, but it took me until I was an adult to admit that when you are organically placed in your element, you just become a stronger version of yourself. I was a better version of myself in an environment that I was not knowingly familiar with long before I knew my fate. I know I am blessed to have experienced this peculiar world since yesteryear is now entombed in Hollywood Forever Cemetery.

The one question I would have asked would be "Who did ya hook up with?" What I would do for Joseph Cotton and Gary Cooper!

I had no idea that fateful blue-sky day, hop-walking to class would shape my life up to now. My dear friend Vinny Pastore (aka Big Pussy in *The Sopranos*) said to me two weeks before I moved to LA, "Our path is already designed for us, Alexis." I didn't understand his cryptic words while eating ice cream on City Island, or know this would be the last time I would have this type of a moment with him.

Boy, was he right!

What can I say? Horror is like the Mafia. "Just when I thought I was out, they pull me back in." But what really sums up the horror genre is Robert De Niro, playing Jimmy "The Gent" Conway in *Goodfellas*, when he grabs the license of a hot truck from a driver: "You might know who we are, but we know who you are."

I was barely unpacked from my life-changing move when I was invited by David Schow to his book signing of *The Outer Limits* at Creature Features in Burbank. Not really knowing about the horror genre, I entered Creature Features on a gloomy night. As I opened the door, my childhood stared right in my face. Fay Wray memorabilia was everywhere. As I approached David's table, he quickly pointed to a group of people gathering in a small circle. I walked up to them, who I now know as close friends and colleagues. I don't know why I did it, but I felt comfortable telling these strangers my Fay Wray secret. When the secret came out, screenwriter/artist Frank Dietz approached me from this unfamiliar crowd and asked me to kindly repeat my story.

If you believe in timing and have the same crush and heartbreak as I do for Kong, you will certainly appreciate the homage documentary that I participated in, directed by Frank Dietz and Trish Geiger, called *Long Live the King*, where I discuss my professional and private life experiences with Fay Wray, along with Joe Dante (director of *Gremlins*), Peter Jackson (*Lord of the Rings*), Greg Nicotero (*The Walking Dead*) and, last but not least, Felissa Rose, my ginzo sister from another mister!

This is a shout out to all modernized, independent women who are too proud to be saved.

Allow men to climb the Empire State building for us, but best be sure you reciprocate that love right back!

And for all of you men who are afraid of feelings and have been easily hurt by women:

Get over it. Grow a pair. Stop "liking" and "tweeting." Shut off your phones and watch *King Kong*. You might learn a thing or two.

You can fight all you want in your social media rants, but you can't fight love.

From the make-believe minds of Merian C. Cooper and Edgar Wallace, King Kong's unstained heart is the size of his hands.

This is my love letter to the 12-year-old girl who was swept up in Fay Wray's hand, taken under her wing and became her friend in real life.

With love,
Alexis Iacono

BLACK CHRISTMAS (1974)

BY
DICK GRUNERT

Writer
Adventure Time, Bunnicula, Yabba Dabba Dinosaurs
Instagram: @DGrunert74 Twitter: @DGrunert

I don't remember the first time I saw *Black Christmas*, but I'll never forget the first time I heard of it.

As a wee lad growing up in the Midwest, I was obsessed with movies (hell, I still am). My entire family (parents, grandparents, aunts and uncles) were huge film buffs, so I guess it was inevitable that I became one, too. I was especially fascinated by horror movies. Thankfully, my parents loved them as well, and they never told me I couldn't watch something. So I was exposed to a lot of pretty hardcore films at an inappropriately early age. I'm lookin' at you, *Last House on the Left*…

Anyway, I devoured every horror movie I could get my eyeballs on, obsessively read *Fangoria* and *Cinefantastique*, and, this being the age before the Internet, religiously watched *Sneak Previews with Siskel and Ebert* to hear about the latest horror flicks coming out (which they usually relegated to the "dog of the week" segment of their show). I was a huge nerd for monster movies and special FX, but more than anything, I loved being scared. So one day, I asked my parents what the scariest movie they ever saw was. Now, you'd expect them to say *Psycho* or *The Exorcist*, but instead they said *Black Christmas*. They told me it was about a crazed serial killer knocking off a bunch of young women inside their sorority house just before Christmas break. The killer, known as "Billy," would make prank phone calls to the sorority after every kill. Sounds cool, but what made it so scary? And that's when my dad dropped the bombshell of all bombshells: Billy was hiding inside the attic the whole time! Don't worry, this isn't a spoiler – it's literally revealed in the very first scene. My prepubescent mind was blown.

I needed to see this movie as soon as humanly possible.

Of course, this being around 1980 B.N. (Before Netflix), I had to wait for the film to be released on home video and then had to wait for my local video store to get it (kids these days have no idea how hard we had it). I don't remember how long that took, but when I finally did see it, the film did not disappoint. From the killer's terrifying prank phone calls to the haunting final shot, *Black Christmas* scared the bejeezus out of me. What I didn't get until years later is just how funny the movie is, thanks to director Bob Clark's expert direction and the very grounded performances from the entire cast, especially Margot Kidder, John Saxon and Doug McGrath as the wonderfully dim-witted desk sergeant Nash. Unlike most horror movies, every single character gets a moment to shine. They feel like real people, not generic victims in a dumb slasher film. Don't get me wrong, I love dumb slasher films, but I knew this movie was something special.

Over the years, I've shown it to many friends. In high school, I was asked to bring a scary movie to the drama club's Halloween party. I brought *Black Christmas* and giggled gleefully as my friends jumped, screamed and gasped throughout the film. One of the girls at that party told me years later that she never went into her attic alone after that. Mission accomplished!

I revisit *Black Christmas* every year, and I catch something new each time, whether it's the brilliant editing, the expert sound design, or the chilling score. This movie is literally the gift that keeps on giving! I've been lucky to see it in a theater, I'm pretty sure I have every DVD and Blu-ray release, I own the soundtrack on vinyl and I even have the paperback novelization! So yeah, this is without a doubt my favorite horror movie.

You're probably wondering what I think of the 2006 remake. I'm no remake snob, but I just couldn't bring myself to watch *Black X-mas* when it came out. I actually watched it for the first time just a couple of years ago…and I liked it. It's nowhere near as good as the original, but it's fun and gory and beautifully shot, and I totally get why it's garnered a bit of a cult following in recent years. It's also ironic that as I write this, Blumhouse just announced a new remake coming out later this year. I look forward to seeing what they do, and I'm happy that young moviegoers might be curious enough to seek out and watch the original.

So, I'd like to thank my parents for telling me about this incredible film all those years ago. Hopefully someday, I'll be able to pass this film on to my kids when they ask me "Hey, Dad…what's the scariest movie you ever saw?"

THE SHINING (1980)

BY

ALEX VINCENT

Actor/Writer/Producer
Child's Play I & II, Curse of Chucky, Cult of Chucky
Instagram/Twitter: @Alex_Vincent
AlexVincentOnline.com AVProductionsOnline.com

When I was asked to write about my favorite horror film, only one answer came to mind. Despite starting my acting career by starring in what has become one of the top horror franchises, I am actually not the biggest horror fan. Perhaps being in a horror film at such a young age has desensitized me to the thrill of being scared from movies, or perhaps growing up as Chucky's best friend has left me uneasily frightened...but the visceral reaction that many horror fans experience has been slightly lost on me. Having worked in film for much of my life I often find myself dissecting the behind-the-scenes aspects to most movies I watch. This approach to the experience isn't very helpful, particularly in horror films where blood, gore, and violent deaths are crucial to the film's impact. I often find myself looking past the brutality to examine the practical effects, prosthetics, and movie magic at play. My best experiences with film are the pictures that can captivate my attention enough to distract me from analyzing the production and leave me engulfed in the story. For that reason, a great horror film has to provide quality acting, suspenseful writing, and deep story telling to make an impact. No horror film has been more successful in those terms to me than *The Shining*. Having never read the book, I did not have any expectations nor previous knowledge of what would unfold.

I remember the first time I saw *The Shining*. I was mesmerized by the deliberate pace and crescendoing suspense. Jack Nicholson delivers one of the most powerful performances in any film ever, not just horror. His descent into madness is so compelling that he takes the viewer along with him through his intense downward spiral. The imagery and dialogue is as instantly riveting as it is permanently memorable. Some of Jack's monologues are so well acted and delivered that I can't help but laugh at times, not because there is anything funny about it, but because it's just that damn good. From the staircase scene to the ax through the door, some of the best lines in horror history get delivered expertly by one of the best actors of our lifetimes. The movie is instantly quotable. The supporting cast is also tremendous. Shelley Duvall is so convincing in her terror that she makes Jack all the more horrifying. This is also one of those films that I can never turn off when I stumble across it. Every viewing feels as enthralling as the first...which is extra satisfying considering there is so much symbolism and hidden meaning scattered throughout. Every time I watch it, I notice something new. As many times as I've seen this film, it never fails to impress me. About once a year or so, someone will approach me at a horror convention and ask why I don't have any photos of *The Shining* at my table. For some reason, despite being born a year after its release, some people are confused into thinking I also played Danny in addition to Andy. Perhaps it's the very common bowl haircut of the '80s. Well, I wish they were correct, because I would have absolutely loved portraying that role!

WATERSHIP DOWN (1978)

BY
MATT OSWALT

Writer/Photographer
Mystery Science Theater 3000, Liquor Stores and Detours
Twitter: @MattOswaltVA Instagram: @MattOswaltVA
MattOswaltPhoto.com

Tasked to write an essay about a horror film that had a huge impact on me, I immediately thumbed through my mind's call caddy of terrifying movies I saw as a child. I started with the edited-for-television versions of *Jaws* and *The Exorcist*, then onto a grainy VHS tape of *The Texas Chain Saw Massacre*, and finally the memory of sneaking into the last half of *Halloween* at our local theater. Each one accomplished its goal: scaring the bejesus out of me and instilling a healthy fear of oceans, religion, and Donald Pleasence that have stayed with me today.

But there was another film that had a much more profound impact on me, and unlike the ones I mentioned, this wasn't a horror movie nor did it intend to terrify me the way it did; all the more reason why it was so damn effective. Linda Blair's spinning head and Leatherface's chainsaw dance were no match for a bunch of animated bunny rabbits.

I'm talking about the 1978 film *Watership Down*.

I grew up in a friendly suburban neighborhood and, every Saturday night over the summer of my eighth year, the local community center would screen outdoor movies. Kids would sit in the grass and watch G-rated fare like *The Apple Dumpling Gang* and *The Sound of Music*. To this day, I'm not sure if the adults who chose *Watership Down* knew what it was or if they just thought it was an animated movie with cute fuzzy "wabbits" and figured it's suitable for all ages. This is the same community center that ran the town pool which featured a high dive that at least one kid every summer fell off and shattered their femur, yet was never removed. So there's a very good chance some dark force lurked in our small bedroom community that took pleasure in ruining our childhoods.

Up until that point I had been weaned on animation that brought a sense of joy, humor, and violence to my imagination. So as the title crawl began with a pleasant shot of the English countryside, I immediately let my guard down and settled in for 90 minutes of sing-songy bunnies in a world of happy colors and warm sentiments. But, without warning, the story took the red brick road into a harsh mythology. It introduced us to the Lord Frith retaliating against the rabbit prince El-ahrairah for disobedience by creating predators with sharp claws and blood-stained fangs to slaughter El-ahrairah's people. It was an uncompromising power-point presentation about fascism, religion, and mortality, with nightmarish images of death.

The political and philosophical metaphors were way over my head, but the relentless bloodletting was enough to hook me in. It was the first time I had seen blood portrayed in cartoon-form. For a child, this is a hell of a lot more horrific than some half-naked teenager running through the woods being pursued by some goof in a hockey mask. The latter is just spectacle, over-the-top gore that immediately desensitizes whatever emotions it stirs up until you become numb to it by the third act. Scary, certainly, but it didn't linger in my subconscious like the raw unfiltered opening scene that rolled out like *Fantasia* directed by Tobe Hooper. That's the stuff that burrows deep into you and remains. For me, that's real horror.

I sat there criss-cross applesauce with my little eyes peeled wide open. I'm well aware that even the tamest animated films subtly deal with death, but at least Bambi didn't stick around to watch the hunters slice her mom from skull to anus and field dress her right there in the meadow. I probably watched the Road Runner effectively 'murder' the coyote over and over, but we never saw it decomposing in the desert while being eaten by buzzards. I was used to death as a punchline or a plot device. *Watership Down* did not hold back. While Disney handled death like the ear-cutting scene from *Reservoir Dogs*, *Watership Down* was the first movie that didn't pan away.

I haven't seen *Watership Down* in probably 20 years, yet even to write this article I didn't need to screen it to refresh my memory. I can still close my eyes and picture the scenes of rabbits being buried alive in the warren, a Rottweiler ripping a slow-footed hare apart like a chew toy, the close-up of General Woundwort's bloody lips and crooked maw right after disposing a foe.

Even the soundtrack left an impact. In the pantheon of terrifying scores, we have *Psycho*, *Halloween*, and *Jaws* but for me, Art Garfunkel's somber ode to death, "Bright Eyes," still haunts me. You could hum the Jaws theme while I'm clinging to a piece of driftwood off Cape Cod and I'd probably join in, but if I'm on my way to Baskin-Robbins on a bright sunny day and "Bright Eyes" suddenly comes on Sirius Radio's '70s on 7, my spine will chill and a cloud of doom will hover over me until it's over.

Guillermo del Toro calls *Watership Down* a "rite of passage," and I prefer to look at my first viewing of it that way rather than to say I was traumatized by it. The older I got, the more I realized that the film hooked me on the power of cinema. I think every cinephile can recall the first movie that challenged instead of placated them. From that moment on, I was more wary and a bit more savvy about what I watched - but it also helped shape my eclectic taste in films.

I think my family got our first VCR in 1985. Cable didn't reach us until a year later, and soon after, the first video store in our town opened, Erol's Video, a quaint east coast video rental franchise. By then, *Watership Down* was deep in my subconscious. It was a conversation with my English teacher that awoke the imagery of rabbits lying in a blood soaked field from their long hibernation. My teacher, while a fan of the book, had never seen the movie and thought my description of its graphic violence was the result of sniffing magic markers in detention, but I insisted my memories were dead on accurate. She agreed to screen it in class if I could get a copy, but that proved harder than I thought.

Erol's, which was a bit like Blockbuster Video's born-again stepmother, didn't carry such films. Their curtained off "Adult" section, which I finally got the nerve to sneak into when the clerk was looking the other way, contained nothing but teenage sex comedies like *The Last American Virgin* and *Porky's*. Even the Woodstock documentary was back there, although in all fairness, those images of Sha Na Na were not suitable for children.

Fortunately, a Tower Records opened a little further down the road. They also rented videos, and after calling them, they confirmed that yes, they had a copy of Watership Down for rent in their...(cue David Lychian music sting)...cult section.

I rented *Watership Down* and my teacher screened it in class. Once again, I fell under its spell and it did its job - basically bummed out everyone in my freshman English class, like playing Kansas' "Dust in the Wind" at a kegger. At this point, I understood the political and religious undertones a lot more, so discovering these new layers only heightened the tension and confirmed how brilliant this movie was to exist on so many levels. And it still frightened the hell out of me, tightening a knot in my stomach the moment Fiver sees a vision of the meadow filling with blood.

I also realized something that made me respect the movie even more. *Watership Down* isn't dark for the sake of being dark. It's just honest. I make this distinction out of respect for Richard Adams, the author of the book the film is based on. To categorize his work as shock or horror would be an insult to his vision. Maybe it's the era in which it was made (the 1970s, one of the best decades of cinema, known for its directors that took artistic risks in storytelling) that allowed a movie like *Watership Down* to exist. So many genres, from westerns to crime films to war movies were deconstructed by the great auteurs of that decade. It stands to reason that an animated film for kids should flip traditional storytelling on its head.

During my teen years I saw pretty much every *Friday the 13th/Nightmare on Elm Street/Evil Dead/Hellraiser* movie, but none had as much impact on me as *Watership Down*. I'll end this essay with a list of the films I discovered at Tower Records, none of which I would have known about if not for following *Watership Down* down the rabbit hole; some horror, some weird, some silly, yet together, all important ingredients in my taste in movies.

El Topo
Pink Flamingos
Desperate Living
Pretty much every Russ Meyer movie (forgive me, I was a teenager)
Wizards
Withnail and I
Eraserhead
A Boy and his Dog
Harold & Maude
Scum
Aguirre, the Wrath of God

Attack of the Killer Tomatoes
Two-Lane Blacktop
The Sinful Dwarf
Don't Look Now
The Groove Tube
Blow-Up
The Long Good Friday
Straw Dogs
Street Trash
Suspiria
Salesman
The Decline of Western Civilization
The Tin Drum
Carnival of Souls
Eating Raoul
The Born Losers
Freaks
Death Race 2000
Henry: Portrait of a Serial KIller

FREDDY'S DEAD: THE FINAL NIGHTMARE

BY

RICKY DEAN LOGAN

Actor

Freddy's Dead: The Final Nightmare,

Back to the Future Part II, Back to the Future Part III

RickyDeanLogan.com Instagram: @RickyDeanLogan

What's my favorite horror movie?

This is a question I get asked a lot. I'll be honest, I was never a horror movie fan growing up. It wasn't until my appearance as Carlos in the sixth *A Nightmare on Elm Street* movie, *Freddy's Dead: The Final Nightmare,* that I fell in love with the horror genre. And not for the reasons you may think.

For instance, the films themselves (which I have learned to love) are not the main reason for my newly found love of the horror genre. It is the horror community itself.

The dedication of horror supporters is what I embrace the most. It still amazes me that the role I did 28 years ago in this amazing franchise is still touching people and loved around the world. Being able to travel the world and meet all my supporters in person is what I really love.

I'm always touched when I hear how my role as Carlos, who had a hearing disability, has inspired so many young hearing impaired lives when *Freddy's Dead* was released. I have these kids, who are now adults, come to my table at conventions and tell me how Carlos helped them to get through a difficult time in school. They say that because I chose to play Carlos without the stereotypical speech impediment and focus on him as a kid who is just like everyone else, I had helped them be seen as normal and even cool. I have to say, I was not expecting that response. I thought it would be more like they would say "I couldn't wear my aid because I was afraid of it turning into a monster!" But instead, they would show me mad love for helping to make their journey easier!! I am so grateful that I was able to touch people in such a positive way.

So to answer the question, "What is my favorite movie?" I would have to proclaim with total sincerity and extreme pride, *Freddy's Dead: The Final Nightmare*! I'm extremely grateful to be part of this iconic franchise.

Being able to work alongside the man himself, Robert Englund, was incredible. Having him declare that Carlos is his favorite kill of the franchise is a true honor. With that, I would truly like to thank all my supporters. I hope to see you soon at a city near you. Lastly, don't forget to use your GPS because, "The Map Says You're Fucked!!"

EVIL DEAD II

BY

MEDUSA MIDNIGHT

Horror Host/Writer/Collector

Attic Vision

Instagram/YouTube: @Medusa_Midnight

For someone like myself, the question "What is your favorite horror movie?" is quite the difficult one, usually resulting in an entire discussion and a small list being made. Within my earliest memories, I can recall watching black and white atomic and Kaiju flicks while my parents attempted to get me to not sit quite so close to the television set, even tossing the occasional house slipper toward my head. I can remember being pre-K and having an utter fascination with 1958's *The Blob.* So just imagine my dismay when I discovered there was a modernized version from 1988 (let's keep in mind there was no such thing as the internet yet). My family had just suffered a fire that consumed our home and forced us to move into a cabin that my father was in the process of building. I went from living next to a highway on the outskirts of a sizable town to the absolute wilderness. My constant during this time was horror. I would stay *Up All Night* watching Gilbert Gottfried and Rhonda Shear. I had a total crush on *Swamp Thing* and would sit cross legged on my parent's brilliant green shag carpet eating ice cream until I couldn't keep my eyes open any longer (which was usually far past the adult's bedtime). To say the least, my parents (and all of their quirks) were easy going. My father had a respectable and odd VHS collection of horror flicks that I would rummage through regularly, reading the backs and dissecting every detail of their artwork. His westerns were off limits of course, unless he was the one putting them in the VCR. He would sit in the same avocado-colored leather chair and drink out of his 'I Love Fishing' coffee cup while we watched movies together. This was the setting for the first time I watched the *Evil Dead* movies.

Evil Dead II is my favorite horror movie. Now don't get me wrong, *The Evil Dead* is truly an almost faultless horror flick. The characters are perfect together, the set-up flows quite beautifully and the atmosphere is perfect, but my fondness for the second installment puts it just a hair ahead of the first. If viewed by itself, without prior knowledge of the universe, one may be somewhat confused. Absolutely zero time is wasted getting into the action. I mean, the entire journey to the cabin, the playing of the tape, the Deadite possession of Linda, and her following execution and burial is all captured within the first 20 minutes of the film. Around this mark, we get what I like to call the memory maker: Linda's dance. My father and I would watch this movie and laugh uncontrollably every single time like we'd never seen it, much less like we had watched it multiple times that very week. Linda's dance scene had to be rewound time and time again so that I too could dance around the living room, acting as though I was rolling my head around gracefully like a ballerina with a basketball. My dad would howl and clap, I would bow, and Linda would disappear into the sky.

The first 20 minutes are what I consider to be some of

the most theatrically beautiful scenes in horror movie history. When Ash is desperately trying to keep himself in one unpossessed piece while actually becoming more and more unglued, having being turned Deadite just moments earlier (and of course lopping off his girlfriend's head with a shovel), his attempted escape is thwarted by the bridge. Bruce Campbell as Ash, stands at the edge of this insane cliff, as the metal bridge we saw intact just moments prior is now in the shape of a menacing claw. Sam Raimi's directorial decisions for this scene are pure genius. Every moment of Ash's struggle, from dismembering Linda and obtaining the chainsaw, to the battle with his possessed hand, absolutely fascinated me as a child. Really, they still do. Bruce Campbell's ability to carry so much of this movie by himself is spectacular.

I've always been infatuated with creature design. Norris in *John Carpenter's The Thing*, and Tarman in *The Return of the Living Dead* are both iconic and beloved, but nothing has resonated like Henrietta and the Deadite tree. Henrietta's several forms are more appealing than the next, especially when trapped in the cellar surrounded by the bubbling pool of blood that was once the character Jake. When the tree uproots and Henrietta is unleashed, allowing the viewer to see the extent of the character (thank you, Ted Raimi), it always makes my heart speed up a bit. The final act of this film is genuinely impressive. These elements throughout *Evil Dead II* make it so alluring and come together perfectly.

A handful of years after our cabin in the wilderness was complete and Joe Bob began hosting *MonsterVision* (I was well on my way of becoming a horror movie connoisseur), my father got sick. Our viewings of *Evil Dead II* never failed to bring us together and induce fits of laughter even when things got to be their worst. When he died in the late 90's, my father left his VHS collection and his love of horror to me. I will always be beholden to the memories that this movie has given me. *Evil Dead II: Dead by Dawn* will always remain at the tip-top of my list, as ever changing as that list may be. When I pop the Vestron Video VHS copy of *Evil Dead II* into my VCR, the trailer for the crime drama *China Girl* plays (a trailer that I know every word of but have yet to see the movie), the Rosebud Releasing screen appears, and I feel at home again.

THE NIGHT STALKER (1972)

BY

LONDON MAY

Actor/Musician/Producer
Samhain, Tiger Army, Son Of Sam,
Brutal Realty Inc., The Tension Experience, Verotika
LondonMay.com BrutalRealtyFilm.com
Facebook: @LondonMayFanPage

Dear horror fans,
Here is a story about my favorite horror film, *The Night Stalker.*
It's all 100% true. I have confessed this to very few people.
I hope you will read it with a grin, a guffaw, and some understanding.
Sincerely,
London May

When Darren McGavin died 13 years ago I was crushed. At the impressionable age of five, I had become obsessed with his role as Kolchak in *The Night Stalker,* when it first aired in 1972. Carl Kolchak was my monster fighting hero and he became my surrogate TV dad who inspired me to be curious, fearless, and rebellious. The show didn't run long, but its effects on me were profound. Growing up, I searched out every article and mention of the show and waited patiently for re-runs. Since there was no internet back then, I mostly had to rely on my imagination as to Kolchak's whereabouts and his future adventures. Kolchak's legacy grew in my head and I, in turn, became a news hound, devouring publications from all over the world, always hoping for a mention of the show or, better yet, a mention of some bizarre unexplained event. I even had serious aspirations of becoming a reporter or detective. And in the true spirit of Kolchak, I hoped I would be fighting monsters at the same time. The closest I got was a paper route, but I never stopped believing.

I, of course, also followed Darren McGavin's non-Kolchak career over the next few decades and enjoyed his other iconic roles. But because I had somehow connected with his grumpy straw hat-wearing persona in my formative years, he was always burned into my brain as Carl Kolchak. The advent of VHS and the underground horror fan community helped keep *The Night Stalker* spirit alive for me as I got older and I valued my 10th generation bootleg videos more than anything. I even handmade my own Kolchak T-shirts which excited a few, but generally confused the majority. (Most people thought it was a picture of George Bush!)

I was 38 when Darren McGavin died in 2006. I had not thought about Kolchak in a while since I was busy with life and what not. Reading about his death sparked something unexpectedly primal and rebellious in me. For years, I had been playing it safe and was settling into a boring domestic life. My friends glazed over when I talked about my passion for a fictional monster-fighting reporter and they were confused at the sadness I felt over the death of a man I had never met. Technically, they were right, but I had grown up under his inspiration and indeed felt the loss. Not only did he instill within me a David vs. Goliath attitude towards evil, he also had emboldened me with a spirit of social activism. Years before, in 2003, I had even embarked on my own real life Kolchak adventure when I bravely investigated a series of under-reported demonic killings in the hopes of becoming a documentary filmmaker and alerting the world to shocking injustices. It was totally reckless and dangerous in hindsight but I thought Kolchak would be proud of my moxie. Besides putting my life at risk, I spent a lot of time and money chasing this modern day "Ripper," but eventually got scooped by a bigger organization who "solved" the case. Of course, the "official story" failed to mention all the supernatural elements that had originally drawn me to the case. Kolchak's famous mantra of "it couldn't happen here" never rang more true.

I knew Darren McGavin's funeral would be my first and last chance to properly pay my respects to Kolchak. I had to act fast, and since public details were scarce, I had to summon up some classic Kolchak ruses to make it happen. My friends rolled their eyes while I called around to all the major Los Angeles cemeteries in a nonchalant and official sounding tone asking what time the McGavin service was. I felt Carl wink at me from somewhere beyond when indeed an operator at Hollywood Forever unknowingly gave up the details to his private ceremony. The game was afoot!

I suited up appropriately in black and called in sick to work the morning of March 5, 2006. I arrived at the gates of Hollywood Forever uninvited and alone since my pals understandably wanted no part in this strange mission. I told the gate guard I was visiting another part of the cemetery and he waved me through. I parked my cruddy Astro Van far away, walked back to the memorial chapel, strolled up the steps confidently and approached the doorman. He gave me that gracious "sincere condolences" face and I stepped inside. I found a seat in the back of the small chapel and tried to play it cool. It was on the early side so I had the whole pew to myself. It was a simple setup but it took my breath away. McGavin lay front and center and I recognized *Night Stalker* cast members Jack Grinnage and Carol Ann Susi quietly paying their respects casket-side.

It was a somber and profound moment and I felt incredibly fortunate and moved to have witnessed it. I was reflecting on McGavin's powerful legacy when a young man plopped his coat down next to me and introduced himself. "Hey, I'm Scotty. Would you save this spot for Peter?" I nodded and acted casual. "Of course." He left but I was internally panicking. I had done the quick math and was sure to be outed when Ralphie from *A Christmas Story* (Peter Billingsley) would soon take a seat next to me and draw a blank at my unfamiliar face.

As the chapel started to fill, I knew I had to move fast if I wanted to have a one to one moment with my hero, Carl Kolchak, before being thrown out on my ass. Jack and Susi had returned to their seats. I rose and strolled reverently to the casket and gazed at the body of Darren McGavin with respect, dignity, and gratitude. I thanked him and told him how much his work meant to me and the positive effect it had on my life. It was a surreal moment and I wanted so bad to touch his hand in comfort, but I refrained. I took a deep breath and returned to my seat, which was now next to the recently arrived "Ralphie," and the other grown up kids from *A Christmas Story*. They had all seen me at the coffin and must have sensed I had some connection to Darren, so they made me feel accepted and sweetly introduced themselves. As I sat next to Peter I quietly told him that he had brought me a lot of joy and laughter from his work with Darren and he thanked me and squeezed my hand. We all sat quietly while Jack and others spoke. When the service was over we filed out and I felt brave and bold enough to even sign the guest register.

There was an intermission before the graveside service and I couldn't decide whether to stay or get the hell out while I was ahead. The option to simply go home and explain all this to my baffled friends just seemed like torture, so I milled about undetected with the other mourners and then decided to double down and proceed to the grave site. Things at graveside seemed to proceed in customary fashion as I watched from the back. Thankfully I have not been to enough burials to be an expert on funeral etiquette, but after the coffin was lowered into the ground there was a final ritual that I was unfamiliar with. A shovel was produced and a select line of mourners queued up to scoop up a mound of dirt and toss it on his lowered coffin.

I watched in awe. This special act seemed powerful and fitting for a man like Carl Kolchak. Even though I was too scared to touch him earlier, I was overtaken at this moment - and I stepped up to join his family and closest friends in this deeply private and personal tribute.

I believe I was the last in line - and that seemed fitting. I was trembling since I had noticed a few quizzical looks as I approached, so I mustered all my Kolchak bravado as I confidently kicked the shovel deep into that mound and got a hefty pound of dirt when it was my turn. As I had seen others do, I didn't look down after I chucked the scoopful on top of his coffin. I wanted so badly to get a final glimpse of Darren but I didn't want to blow my cover. I simply planted the shovel back in the dirt, respectfully bowed my head and quietly moved back to the edge of the small crowd. It was probably my imagination, but I felt the energy shift and the crowd seemed to separate a bit as I walked through, as though they sensed I was not one of them. I felt a wave of exhilaration and then a sudden typhoon of shame, so I retreated back to my van. I kept waiting for an angry "Hey you!" or a security officer to intercept me but it never happened. Driving home, I felt like I had taken it too far and I immediately regretted the whole thing. Had I been disrespectful to a man and his family at their most vulnerable moment? I wondered what and why the hell I did what I did to a man I had greatly respected and admired like a father. I wanted to be brave and bold like Kolchak, but now I was more depressed than ever. If anyone close to his family ever reads this I apologize for intruding. I got carried away with selfish grief and desperation. Kolchak will always be my hero, and my heart still pumps with his spirit of monstrous curiosity, equality, and truth. I just don't do it at funerals anymore. Over the years, I have, on numerous occasions, privately visited Darren

McGavin's grave site to reflect on all of this. I hope he's forgiven me.

THE TEXAS CHAINSAW MASSACRE 2
BY
JOE KNETTER

Writer
Blind, Desert Moon, Twisted Loneliness, Room
Facebook: @Joe.Knetter Instagram: @JoeyKnetter

In 1986, I was ten years old and lived in a small town in Minnesota named Eyota. I was a shy kid and, I'll admit, a little odd. I loved horror. I gobbled up as much as I could, and food too, which is how I went from a skinny kid to a chubby fuck over one summer. It's hard moving to a new town in the summer and having no friends. But we don't need to talk about that here other than mentioning that I have lost 75 pounds this year and I'm looking sexy as hell. I ooze machismo. My friend Steve Barton has joined me on this weight loss attack and we are both sexifying California, especially on our weekly radio show *Brainwaves: Horror and Paranormal Talk Radio* which airs Wednesday at 7pm on the Deep Talk Radio Network. Boom, plugged the shit out of that and it wasn't forced. It just came naturally, just like horror did for me. Boom, right back to the story.

Luckily for me, I was surrounded by relatives that supported my love of horror. Uncle Mike would always take me to see whatever was in the theatre. He also took me to comic book stores and my favorite thing to pick up was *Fangoria Magazine*. I read each issue cover to cover many times before I cut out my favorite pictures and taped them to my walls. At that point in my life, I had the entire second floor of the house to myself. I had a bathroom and two small bedrooms, but the best thing was the walk-in closet that was between them. As far as walk-in closets go, it wasn't much, but I was much smaller then so it was downright cavernous to me. The cool thing was that, behind the clothes hanging on a pole was an area about six feet by four feet. It was hidden by the clothes. This was my special place. This is where I decided to erect a shrine to horror. I called it my horror Hall of Fame. Most of the pictures I put on my walls went in there. My friend Dylan and I would spend countless hours talking about horror in there. On a side note, Dylan's younger brother now plays drums for the band Ministry. How batshit insane is that? He always loved music so it's wonderful to see him chasing and achieving his dream. Life is amazing. Anyway, back to the past.

It was while reading the new issue of *Fangoria* that I came to an article on a new movie that would be coming out soon. I read that sucker twenty or thirty times. Tom Savini was going to do the effects and he was the master as far as I was concerned. I just knew it was going to be the greatest movie ever. Sometime later, while watching TV at my Nana's house, I got my first look at the trailer. I can clearly remember playing with my *Star Wars* toys and realizing what was on the TV behind me. I turned around and was captivated from the moment it began. Seeing these moving images reinforced my belief that this would be something special. The trailer ended and I was in heaven. It was everything I had been waiting for. I played with my toys in front of the TV for hours, waiting for it to play again. I needed to see it from the beginning since I had missed the opening. I waited and waited, no doubt allowing the rancor to devour Luke and Han since I was always drawn to the dark side and the monsters that existed within. My patience paid off. It played again...and I was devastated. The trailer opened with a warning that no one under the age of seventeen would be allowed in the theatre. I'm not ashamed to admit that I cried. I would not be able to see it for seven years. Remember, I was ten at the time and, since it carried this warning, I was sure video stores wouldn't carry it. It would only be rented at the porn shops. Uncle Mike was cool as fuck, but I knew he wouldn't go to a porn shop to rent a movie for me, even if it was a horror film. So I cried and did my best to carry on. *TCM2* would be in more *Fangoria* issues and it would reopen the wound every time. I had to come to terms with it even though it broke my little horror heart. Time passed, though the longing never diminished. On the weekends, Uncle Mike would take me to the local Cub Foods grocery store to rent movies. Back then, you could rent videos everywhere. Grocery stores, gas stations...you name it. It was a wonderful time full of discovery. Most would consider puberty to be like that. For me though, it was video stores. Renting movies based on cover art was magical. It's something that is lost to time and will never come back. Now, you know everything about a movie before it comes out. It's rare to just discover something. I miss it so much, but am thankful that I grew up in the time to fully experience and appreciate it.

It was on one of these trips to the video store that I saw it sitting on the shelf. I gasped, unable to believe what I was seeing. *The Texas Chainsaw Massacre 2* was right there in front of me. I reached out for it, but before I could, some dude much older than me snagged it. A fit of rage hit, unlike any I had ever experienced before. I grabbed *Doom Asylum*, the first movie I could reach and proceeded to beat the man to death. I was a wild animal, bone, guts and gore showered the racks. I'm just kidding. *Doom Asylum* didn't come out until the next year. I picked the VHS up off of the shelf and grinned like a madman. I was finally going to see it. We went back home, popped that sucker in, and after all the expectations and build-up, I was not disappointed in the slightest. It was very different than the original, but it had to be. Times had changed. The world had changed.

Yuppie is such a dated term. The current generation has no concept of what a yuppie is. They have hipster down though and I'm not sure which group irks me more. Yuppies had money, dressed like it and surely acted like it. They were better than you in every way, at least that's what they thought. I didn't come from money. I grew up in a trailer court. What we didn't lack was love and the ability to get along with everyone. We didn't need to look down at anyone to feel better. The yuppies of course would say, "You can't look down from the bottom." Not all yuppies were bad people. They were born into an environment that fostered those feelings, just like many people are today. The key is realizing, learning and changing. Some did...some do. The rest of those yuppie fucks? We wished brutal death upon them and that's how the film opens.

Technically the film opens with a crawl just like the original. The original film's crawl gave away the ending, though that never bothered me. Stephen King is fond of saying that it's about the journey, not the destination, and I agree with him for the most part. However, if I was heading to Disneyland and the ride was full of laughs, good food and conversation, but upon arrival was urinated and defecated on by a costumed stranger, I may not reflect on that drive as being positive. The original film backs his claim though. You know from the beginning that Sally will survive and the bad guys will get away, but that doesn't matter. A fantastic movie makes you forget what you know and takes your hand and drags you along. The *TCM2* crawl gives a quick recap of the original before letting the audience know that bodies have continued to show up all over Texas. We know the Sawyer family hasn't gone into hiding. They are out there doing what they do. The difference is, they are mobile. You avoided them by steering clear of their home in the first one. You had to stumble upon it. This time though, you weren't safe from them stumbling upon you.

While the first film opened with some quick flashes, building up the tension and setting the tone, this one sets the mood immediately in a much different way. You see a road before you like many across the country. Suddenly, a gunshot is heard, a mailbox is shot, and we meet the dreaded yuppies. One hangs out the window wearing a pair of ridiculously awful '80s glasses, laughing in an annoyingly awful way while shooting signs. His yuppie pal driving is equally as awful. Many watching now would consider these two as an exaggerated caricature of the '80s. Those of us who lived through that time know that the portrayal is close to what they were: entitled assholes dressed in obnoxious colored sweaters. While the first movie made you feel for the characters and want to see them survive (other than Franklin because...well...he's Franklin), this one does the opposite. You want to see these dickheads die.

The beauty of the original was that you felt like you were there experiencing it. *TCM2* is vastly different. You immediately knew you were watching a movie. It allows you to relax and just relish in what you are seeing. It's okay to smile, it's okay to cheer. This one doesn't rely heavily on ambient noise to help set the scene, you get actual music and songs. Again, it was a product of the times. In the '70s, films were events. The only way to see them was at a theatre. That's why midnight screenings and double features were so prevalent and played to packed houses all across the country. When home video started, you could see movies whenever you wanted, provided it wasn't rented already, and let me tell you that was always a crushing moment. These days, people freak out when the Netflix signal buffers for a second. Back then, you'd have to wait until the next day to check the video store again...and it was always about timing. If they returned the tape early in the day, it would be gone by the afternoon. I remember standing at the checkout counter waiting for a movie to get returned. If you were lucky, you'd see it there waiting to be put out and snag it right from the counter. Movies became rewatchable. You could pause, rewind and dissect them. The best of the classic horror cinema (*Night of the Living Dead, The Texas Chain Saw Massacre* etc.) stood the test of time. Many films that relied on tension and the experience that goes along with it lost some steam after repeated viewings. The way around this was to make films that added a little more fun, gore, and yes, nudity. *TCM2* definitely had the fun and the gore, though there was no nudity. As a ten-year-old, the nudity didn't really matter to me, that would come later... as I would...many times. What I'm getting at is movies for the home market had to be rewatchable in order for you to justify a purchase or multiple rentals. Tobe Hooper and writer L.M. Kit Carson knew this. They also knew that they couldn't make the same style of movie as before. It wouldn't have the impact and they had already made a perfect version. They chose to make this one a black comedy horror film. I know in interviews Tobe Hooper said that the original was a black comedy, but I've never noticed that. It's pure horror to me. So back to the yuppies.

They listen to a radio show and decide to call in. Stretch, the host, played by a wonderful Caroline Williams takes the call and yep, the yuppies are assholes. Let's talk about Caroline for a moment. She's fantastic in this, as she was in every role she played...and somehow...over the years, she went from being good looking to absolutely stunning. I don't know what fountain of youth she bathed in (I would gladly watch that), but she definitely should share her secrets. She carries most of the movie and does it justice. L.G., played by the perfectly cast Lou Perryman plays her engineer. Lou worked in the camera department on the first film so it's great to see him step in front of the camera. He perfectly offsets her beauty with his inherit manliness. Not that spitting should be considered manly, but let's face it, when you're twelve, you go through a time when it's just the coolest thing. I remember hocking loogies everywhere. We immediately like these two. Their chemistry on-screen is great, as is their banter. The yuppies decide to play chicken with a truck driving down the country road and cause the truck to swerve into the ditch. Of course they think this is the funniest thing ever. The call is disconnected and Stretch continues her show. L.G. is crass, gruff and vulgar (sound like anyone you know) and obviously has a crush on Stretch. Though she brushes him off, you can see in her eyes and mannerisms that she likes him. These two really mesh together well. I would have watched another movie with these characters in a heartbeat. He built her a fry house; I would have loved to see a chicken strip cabin. I would eat the fuck out of one of those.

The yuppies call back later and Stretch and L.G. are unable to disconnect the call. Suddenly, the truck from earlier is in front of the kids. They stop, and there's a moment where you can see their shock at not being the ones in charge. They have lived their lives getting everything they want and being kings of the castle. This shift in paradigm confounds them. They have no clue whom they have pissed off, but as an audience, we do, and eagerly anticipate what is coming. That's another core difference between films - the first made you cringe and feel for those being attacked; in the sequel you cheer for the Sawyers. You want bloodshed, and in *TCM2*, you get it in all of its red-soaked glory provided by Tom Savini. There are no tricks to make you imagine what you saw like the hook scene in the original. In this one, you kick a wall and guts come flying out.

So the yuppies take off, trying to get away from the truck. They head down the world's longest bridge and you suddenly get what you want. In the first one, you waited quite a while to get your first glimpse of Leatherface. Here, it comes quickly. (My lady, Sarah French, would like to make a joke here, but I'm not going to let her. That would be rude and not the truth at all. I swear.) Out from the truck pops Nubbins, a member of the Sawyer clan that has seen better days. He's nothing more than a dried-out and dressed corpse. One of the yuppies shoots Nubbins and his head shifts, showing who is disguised underneath. It's our old friend Leatherface, played in this scene by Tom Morga who also portrayed Michael Myers in *Halloween 4* and Jason Voorhees in *Friday the 13th 5*. He does exactly what we want him to do by sawing the shit out of those yuppies. Unfortunately for the Sawyers, they were still being broadcast on the radio. Enter Dennis fucking Hopper.

I love what he brings to the table. It's batshit crazy, no doubt about that. His character, Lefty Enright, has been searching for the Sawyers since his niece and nephew, Franklin and Sally from the original, encountered the clan. He has put everything together and even though no one agrees with him, he knows there are devils on the loose killing at will all across Texas. He will stop at nothing to see them sent back to hell. Casting an actor the caliber of Dennis Hopper was a major score. It brought recognition and some name value. You can't help but smile at every scene he is in . The way he cuts up the logs at the chainsaw store makes me laugh out loud. I also realize that he isn't as far from insanity as he thinks. He has been driven to it, rather than born into it though. He knows his mission will more than likely be a one way trip. The fact that he tosses down more money without care than needed for the chainsaws shows he knows the end is near and he's fully accepted that.

When Stretch reads about Lefty, she knows the tape she has from the show is exactly the people he is searching for. Lefty has her play it on the radio and Drayton "The Cook" Sawyer, played by the returning and utterly fantastic Jim Siedow, hears it on the air. In the fashion of the '80s, the Sawyers now have a rolling BBQ. They crave awards and money, no longer content to just be together and enjoy life. They've monetized cannibalism. His inclusion really connects the two films and it is better because of his involvement. While he adds a touch of class, he's also allowed to go more over-the-top this time and delivers many memorable lines. But if we are going to talk about memorable lines, we have to bring up Chop Top.

Stretch meets Chop Top at the end of the broadcasting day. She stumbles upon him in the lower level of the station. His appearance (head plate and coat hanger), mannerisms and demeanor all reek of crazy. Almost every line he delivers throughout the movie has become quotable and legendary.

"Lick my plate you dog dick."
"Dog will hunt."
"Music is my life."

He is a character that you cannot forget, as is Bill Moseley, the man who brought him to life. The guy is a genius and I'm not just talking about his acting ability. He really is a genius. He went to Yale and wrote for *Omni* magazine. How many people do you know that took their family to a rainforest on vacation? He knows a little bit about everything. I'll share one of my favorite Bill stories with you.

Bill and I were both attending Cinema Wasteland in Strongsville, Ohio. I can't recommend that show enough. Great people, great times. Bill loves nature and likes to go for walks whenever he's in town for an appearance. On this occasion, I joined him. We found a little wooded area behind the hotel and commenced with our stroll. I had known Bill for a few years at this point, but still wondered if he was leading me to my death. He plays the character so damn well and has a way of glossing over his eyes when he's in character that made me wonder. I still went though, because, if I'm going to go, there are worse ways than by Chop Top. So we are walking around and he's pointing out to me what the various plants are and I wonder if he's bullshitting me. Suddenly, he stops, climbs up a tree, picks something off a branch and swings back down. Unbelievable. It still brings a smile to my face. He showed me what he picked and it was some berry, though I don't remember the name. How could I? Fucking Chop Top just pulled a Tarzan.

Chop Top is zany, crazy, deranged and funny as hell. He has a surprise for Stretch hidden in the record room, and that's his bro Leatherface.

Other than the opening scene, Leatherface is played by Bill Johnson and Bob Elmore. The budget allowed for stunt people this go-around. I'm sure the cast of the original would have gladly let people step in for the more heavy stuff. But, that movie would have suffered for it. It needed that pain and anguish.

This one didn't rely on tone as much as it relied on individual performances in order to be memorable.

Leatherface is quite different this time around. No longer is he the worried child; he gets to have some fun, even giving some skin to Chop Top at one point. He has adopted the teenager mentality in the family and is quite horny. *TCM2* is well known for this change. We see a Leatherface that wants to get a piece. The seduction scene with the chainsaw, though creepy as fuck, does come across as slightly erotic. Maybe that's just me though. If it is, my apologies...no fuck that, I love it. This scene is where the movie becomes nuts. From here out, it's full-steam frantic salaciousness, camp, and gorgeous gore. There's a dinner scene, a chainsaw duel, and a skinning.

You can't really compare Gunnar Hansen's portrayal to Bill Johnson's. They were both working with different material and tone. Both did a fantastic job. I'd also like to point out that in real life, both are highly intelligent men that strike me as more Shakespearean than anything. The stories they told, the laughs they had, drew you in and had a way of making you feel more intelligent just being in their presence. It's funny how the monsters are almost always the polar opposite of the people that played them. It's been that way from the beginning with actors like Karloff, Chaney and Price. It takes intelligence to craft a character, especially one that has no lines. It's all told through the eyes and movements.

The set dressing of the Sawyer's lair is quite amazing. Last year, I got to catch a screening in a theatre, something I waited thirty years to do. Every inch of the screen was dressed. There are no gaps, no "fuck it, no one will notice." The attention to detail is astounding. You never feel like you are there like the first film, but you feel like you want to be there. It's a carnival of the grotesque and, as bad as the Sawyers are, you can't help but like them. Rob Zombie was able to do a similar thing with *The Devil's Rejects* and it's no surprise Bill Moseley was also front and center there.

The first *Texas Chain Saw Massacre* is a cinematic masterpiece. Attempting to do another was a disaster waiting to happen. The choices they made with the script and tone of *TCM2* are what saved it. It has a great balance of humor, bizarreness, and horror. It is very much an '80s movie through and through and that's not a bad thing. It knows exactly what it is; there are no delusions of grandeur. Every aspect of it went in a different direction than the previous and it was the right thing to do. In the original, you felt like you were there taking part in their experience. It felt dark and dirty, and left an impact on you in many ways. *TCM2* aims for a different experience. It's a movie meant to be seen with friends. You should laugh and smile along with it. That's what the '80s were about. It's not the greatest horror film and doesn't aim to be. It's there to entertain you and it certainly does.

I was ten and a weird kid living in a small town. I didn't have many friends but I had my monsters. It was the middle of the '80s, which I consider one of the greatest decades in regard to music and movies. This was my movie, the one I anticipated the most and cried over. It was a dangling carrot I couldn't reach. Uncle Mike lifted me up though and allowed me to grab it. He passed away many years ago, but I think of him often. I think of what my life was like during those years. The world was a different place. I think of how different things could have been for me if I didn't have people around me that allowed me to be me. I was a weird kid. I am a weird adult. *TCM2* works because of the smile that exists behind all of the horror. That's something I've always held onto. I write and say some crazy shit, but there is always a hint of a smile lurking there. *The Texas Chainsaw Massacre 2* is my movie. It's me in a nutshell. And that's why it is my favorite film of all time.

ALIEN

BY

ANDREW KASCH

Director/Editor

Never Sleep Again: The Elm Street Legacy,
DC's Legends of Tomorrow, Tales of Halloween

Instagram: @AndrewKasch Facebook: @Andrew.Kasch

I didn't see the chestburster scene the first time I watched *Alien.* Instead, I had a blanket over my head as I heard John Hurt's dying screams along with a bunch of other horrible sounds I couldn't make out. As any veteran horror fan will tell you, this was a huge mistake because the theatre of the mind makes it a hundred times worse. But I was 10. What the hell else do you do when you're 10?

Alien wasn't the first horror movie I saw and by then, I was already a committed genre nerd. I had grown up on Lucas, Spielberg and Dante. *Godzilla* and *King Kong* movies had already turned me into a monster kid. There had been plenty of other "gateway" films, books and TV that gave me my earliest thrills: *Jaws...Scary Stories To Tell in the Dark...The Wolf*

Man...*Return to Oz* (shut up, it's horror!)...*Are You Afraid of the Dark*?...The *It* miniseries (which doesn't hold up, but sent me head first into my love of Stephen King)...the psychedelic nightmare sequences of early Disney movies...but *Alien* was the first film that traumatized me.

I spent my childhood in love with movies, but growing up in the religious South meant that what I could watch was very selective. The genre was still largely forbidden fruit and an older family friend had rented *Alien* on a VHS tape from Blockbuster Video (that was a building you drove to in order to find your movies, millennials). I already knew what the creature looked like from The Great Movie Ride at Disney's Hollywood Studios, but absolutely nothing about the film itself. There was no *Alien* franchise (just the one sequel) and no internet, so the only information came from magazines. I went in totally blind.

I was captivated and terrified right from the opening title sequence. The atmosphere, the creature work, the sets and designs, the raw performances and Jerry Goldsmith's incredible score all felt like a sonic boom to the soul. It was unlike anything I had ever seen and it played entirely against all my expectations. By the time the film iced Tom Skerritt's Dallas (people still forget he was the lead, not Ripley), it was clear this story wasn't playing by any rules.

I had to pause the movie at three different points just to work up the nerve to continue (once after the chestburster, once just before Harry Dean Stanton's death, and once more after Veronica Cartwright's uncomfortable off-screen demise), but eventually made it through. By the time Sigourney Weaver blew the fucker out of the goddamn airlock, I idolized her for life. I popped the VHS out of the player with shaking legs and that night I could barely sleep. When I did, I had nightmares of face-huggers coming for me.

I was hooked.

But it still took me six months to work up the courage to sit through James Cameron's *Aliens*, which regularly aired on HBO in those days. I also watched that film through my fingers, and it completely delivered along with the added dose of adrenaline that appealed to my inner action junkie. I inhaled Cameron's other films and his regular cast of faces introduced me to virtually every great character actor of the '80s and '90s. Lance Henriksen, Bill Paxton, Michael Biehn, Jenette Goldstein...These people became my rock stars.

The same family friend who showed me *Alien* on VHS later took me to see David Fincher's *Alien 3* in theaters. Despite being devastated by certain plot developments (cruel even by today's standards), I enjoyed it...and grew to love it much later on. It wasn't the sequel anyone wanted, but a deep and accomplished film on its own merits (the Extended Cut arguably stands as a masterpiece).

As a kid, my *Alien* obsession continued long past the trilogy. I read the Dark Horse comics, all those cheesy tie-in novels, and even wrote letters to 20th Century Fox. At the dawn of the internet, I would chat on *Alien* messageboards and learn about all the sequels that didn't get made. Like most fans, that love has been severely tested by the installments that came later, but the spirit of those original movies lives on in new and exciting ways - from Sega's brilliant *Alien: Isolation* to the North Bergen High School drama department that staged an *Alien* play.

Together, the one-two punch of *Alien/Aliens* set me on a different path, not just with movies, but exploring how they're made and the craftsmanship that goes into them. I've rewatched both endlessly to the point where I remember every line and marine name, and I still find new details and questions to explore thirty years later. More than any other horror film, they were the two that lit my imagination on fire and made want to get into the industry.

A few years ago, I was lucky enough to be invited to Bob Burns' basement and stood in the middle of virtually every surviving prop from the first two films: the Alien Queen, the Nostromo, Sulaco, the MU/TH/UR 6000 computer, and the very first facehugger, among dozens more...and the experience was overwhelmingly emotional. For me, this is where the art form peaked: they are, in effect, the last great tangible creature features from a living, breathing world that didn't come from a computer. You can feel every speck of creativity put into them from all departments.

I don't have a large memorabilia collection, but above my bed is a giant *Alien* head signed by H.R. Giger. The signature has faded to almost nothing, but it sits there like a biomechanical dreamcatcher and a constant reminder of where that love of creativity comes from. In a town as tough as Hollywood, it's important to hang onto your passions – even if that passion is an angry phallic star beast.

THE GATE

BY

ANTHONY ARRIGO

Assistant Director/Writer

Encounter, Automation, Psycho Granny, Knifecorp, Dread Central

Instagram: @IslandClaws

When it comes to my favorite horror movie, half a dozen candidates fit the bill, nearly all of which earned their place due to that most addictive drug: nostalgia. My first taste of horror came in 1985 or '86, when *Indiana Jones and the Temple of Doom* was playing at a friend's house and I walked into the room just in time to see Mola Ram (Amrish Puri) rip a man's heart from his chest. It could easily have been *The Monster Squad*, which I first saw at an age young enough to continually forget the title despite being in love with the premise. *Evil Dead II: Dead by Dawn* is another contender – after seeing it as "Siskel & Ebert's Video Pick of the Week" I raced down to my local Warehouse, rented the only copy, and watched it over and over for a week. Some memories come in little bursts – pieces of scenes, feelings of dread and abject terror almost completely foreign to my older, jaded self. The ending of *Halloween*; Jason's final showdown with Trish and Tommy in *Friday the 13th: The Final Chapter*; merely looking at Freddy Krueger's face on the VHS art for *A Nightmare on Elm Street Part 2: Freddy's Revenge*. These are the things that bolstered my early love of horror and solidified my place as a lifelong fan. But my favorite? That honor goes to *The Gate* – this is the film that not only introduced me to horror; but, more than that, it takes me back to a specific time and place.

Windsor, Connecticut circa late '80s/early '90s...

Back then, we lived within driving distance of my grandparents' place – a quaint, typical New England home situated on a large plot of land, bordered on the backside by "endless" woods. There was a long, lush patch of green grass out front that I would occasionally get to trim using my grandpa's sitting lawn mower. A massive blackberry bush on one side of the house fed me during the day's adventures. It was my own bucolic paradise. Early in the evening, I would sit with my grandma and mother in the well-lit front parlor, watching new episodes of *Murder, She Wrote* or *The Golden Girls*; however, after family dinner I would usually sneak off onto the back porch where my grandpa would sit, digest and drink in his well-worn cloth La-Z-Boy recliner while watching some R-rated content. Grandpa was known to be a heavy drinker and an equally heavy smoker, and while he wasn't always the most jovial person to be around, he adored me. This was unofficially "our time." The porch was screened-in and dark, nestled right up against those endless woods. The only light source came from the occasional firefly. Everyone else was asleep, the house turned pitch black and foreboding, belying the welcoming atmosphere of the afternoon. There, I got my introduction to horror.

Grandpa flipped on *The Gate* too late for me to catch the title but early enough to get the gist of things. Glen (Stephen Dorff) and his miscreant metalhead buddy Terry (Louis Tripp) unearth a huge geode in Glen's backyard and, naturally, they crack it open, revealing brilliant crystals; but the exterior rolls over to a magnetic doodle pad, revealing arcane incantations. The boys read the words aloud without a second thought before heading downstairs to spy on older sister Alexandra's get-together. Glen's parents are out of town for the weekend and Terry's dad is a hopeless drunk, giving the duo more than enough opportunity for a little light mischief. But when a playful game of levitation turns frighteningly real, with Glen frantically reaching for a light fixture to stop his ascent and Terry having a hallucinatory somnambulist nightmare of his dead mother embracing him in her arms, the boys suspect there was more in that hole than just a geode. The next day, using the cherished wisdom of a heavy metal record – Sacrifyx's The Dark Book (sadly, not real) – Glen and Terry discover the gateway they inadvertently opened can be closed with a simple ritual since a required sacrifice was not yet made to the "Old Gods" down below. What they don't know is that after the family dog, Angus, was found dead following the party last night, one of Alexandra's friends dumped the body into that big hole in her backyard (because you can always count on movie teenagers to be extra lazy).

With the setup complete, the film then showcased what has been etched into my memory since: Randall William Cook's creepy stop-motion creations. I was a creature kid, raised on a daily diet of Showa-era *Godzilla* films, *King Kong* (1933), and the classics of Ray Harryhausen; none of which are outright horror but the elements are certainly present. *The Gate* provided the perfect marriage of monsters and mayhem, set within a tonally dark world where the authority figures to which kids would instinctively turn are nowhere to be found. Diminutive demons terrorize Glen, Terry, and Alexandra from without and within; nowhere is safe. A local legend told by Terry earlier – that of a workman dying within the walls of Glen's home – turns tangible when a decayed body bursts forth from behind its drywall crypt, dragging away a horrified Terry. Later, when that rotting worker returns, Alexandra belts him in the head with a stereo. As his body hits the floor it bursts into a dozen little minions ready for attack. Those minions are merely an amuse bouche for the Big Bad, a gargantuan worm-like demon with myriad eyes and arms. When it touches Glen, an eye appears within the palm of his hand. Blood rains down from the walls. Cook crams creativity into every cranny, making use of stop-motion animation, forced perspective, man-in-suit action, and miniatures to sell the illusion to viewers that nothing is what it seems.

What scared me most - and stuck with me for so many years - were the feelings of hopelessness and dread experienced by these kids. At one point Glen is relieved to see his parents have come home – only these things aren't his parents. "Dad" tries to choke Glen and has his face literally ripped off in the process, all while "Mom" is howling with laughter in the background. The only stability and trust within the trio is in each other, and even that shatters when a demon that looks like Terry attacks Alexandra and Glen later in the film. Home is where children should feel safest. Here, it is used as a gateway for netherworld demons with plans of laying waste to the suburbs and beyond, making Glen's house the least safe place to be. Glen just wanted to shoot off some rockets and mess around in the backyard. Terry just wanted to play heavy metal records and be weird. These simple pleasures of childhood unknowingly unleashed a beast and neither boy knows how to stop it. Glen wants the nightmare to end so he can go back to being a kid – and at the time I found that fairly horrifying: that an idyllic day could somehow become an apocalyptic evening.

The impact horror has on a viewer dulls with experience, something hardcore fans know all too well. When you are a kid, though, and don't yet know "how the sausage is made," that's when horror can make the biggest impact. There isn't any context for that chilling effect; the genre may be full of tropes and tried-and-true terrors, but we all have to see them somewhere for the first time. I look back with laughter on the things that used to scare me. But back then, nestled within the confines of a screened-in patio, surrounded by a dimly moonlit acre of woods where every who-knows-what lurked, I got to experience that chill for the first time as *The Gate* unspooled on late-night television. My grandparents are long since gone, their house is no longer in the family and I haven't even been back to Connecticut in a couple of decades. But I always carry a pair of rose-tinted glasses for the past; some of my favorite memories are sitting back there on the patio, punching above my weight, and watching a few heavies with the old old man. For me, *The Gate* isn't only a killer '80s satanic creature feature, it's a time machine – and it takes me right back to a place that only exists in memories.

THE SHINING (1980)

BY

JEANNE "HOLLYWOOD" BASONE

Professional Wrestler/Stuntwoman/Actor
GLOW, Lollipop Gang, Silent Times,
JAG, Chuck, Days Of Our Lives
JeanneBasone.com Instagram: @OfficialGlowHollywood
Twitter: @GlowHollywood
Facebook: @HollywouldProductions

I've been a professional wrestler since I was 21 years old. The affiliation was called *GLOW*, which stands for *Gorgeous Ladies of Wrestling*. I played a character named Hollywood, half the tag team of Hollywood and Vine. That's a rough intersection, and we were a rough and tough as well! We definitely weren't "Baby Faces" (the "good girls" in wrestling slang). We were definitely "Heels" (the bad girls/guys). In my eyes, those characters were the best ones to play!

The topic of bad girls/bad guys brings me to my favorite horror movie. Picking one "favorite" is going to be tough because there are just way too many that I love!

It all started with a small, used, black-and-white TV my parents put in the bedroom that I shared with my sister. From there, I'd watch every black-and-white horror film that came on Saturday or Sunday matinees. Anything to do with vampires was right up my alley. Here is the interesting thing: at the tender age of 9 or 10, I obviously hadn't thought about a career, much less being a professional wrestler! But what I did know was that when I watched these movies, I wanted the vampire or the bad guy to get away with everything and have his way with his victims. No wonder I wound up taking on the "bad girl" wrestling persona of Hollywood so much!

When I first watched *Nosferatu*, I was completely hypnotized by his character. I mean he totally creeped me out. No hair, completely bald, big ears, and those two large incisors. Yikes! If you've ever had a nightmare about monsters or vampires, you may want to look in the mirror to make sure you don't have any fresh punctures on your neck.

One of the reasons why I once took a low-budget acting class at LA Valley College is the movie *Night of the Living Dead*. What's not to love about this movie? The living dead walking through the cemetery is bone chilling. A zombie chasing Barbara winds up killing her brother. Barbara panics, gets in the car, and of course...she crashes it. She finds the nearest home for safety, but it's just one thing after another. I can't imagine running into a stranger's house, meeting them, and then having living corpses wanting to eat at your flesh. This movie had such an effect on me that I can't help thinking of it every time I drive by a cemetery!

Which brings me back to this memory: going to the 1983 U.S. Festival in Southern California. When the concert was over we couldn't find our friend so we didn't have a way back home. It was after midnight and it was very dark with no streetlights. We walked to a random house, knocked on the door, and asked if we could please use their telephone to call our parents to come pick us up. Now that was a concert!

Halloween has always been one of my very favorite holidays! Of course, as we got a little older and didn't need mom and dad to escort us to the neighbors' houses, we started venturing out a little bit further into neighborhoods we weren't familiar with. Thank goodness in Burbank, pretty much everything was safe during the '70s. The only thing we heard about was to watch out for razor blades in apples! Oh, and my mother always instilled in us that if anyone asked us to take a ride with them, we should say no, turn around, and run the other way!

This takes me back to the original *Halloween* starring Jamie Lee Curtis and makes me think about my teenage babysitting days. One thing that made it so scary was that it was the kind of movie that could happen in my own town. I mean, there's a serial killer going after babysitters just like me! Whenever I hear John Carpenter's *Halloween* theme music, I can always envision Michael in his mask lurking around a dark corner of my house. Oh, and I always check my backseat!

Another slasher film that brings me back to my sweet 16 is *The Texas Chain Saw Massacre*. I saw it with my first boyfriend at the Pickwick, Burbank's local drive-in theater that all the high school kids frequented. True, most of them were drinking beer and having make out sessions, but honest to God, I did watch this movie! I don't think I've ever felt so freaked out and scared as when Leatherface impaled Pam on the meat hook - OMG this guy is an F'n lunatic! And getting impaled on the meat hook must have hurt like hell! I always wondered, if I was in a horror movie, would I trip and fall like most of the damsels in distress do? Hell, no! I'm going to make it out alive!

Carrie and *The Shining* are both based on novels by Stephen King, but I definitely like each movie version better. For *Carrie*, what hits me the most is what is going on in today's world.

Bullying! I remember girls in eighth grade making fun of me because I dated the most popular, good looking guy at our school! Why pick on someone just because a cute boy likes someone else more than he likes you? Stop the needless bullying, people! So, good for Carrie getting her revenge on those jealous insecure twits! And with *The Shining*, it was Jack's insanity that makes him the best "bad guy" ever for me. And when you discover what he is typing over and over ("All work and no play makes Jack a dull boy") you realize this guy has really lost it! Another line that always gets me is, " Wendy, darling, love of my life! I'm not gonna hurt you…I'm just gonna bash your brains in. I'm gonna bash 'em right the f--k in!" Stanley Kubrick totally knew what he was doing when he directed this movie, and that's why - among all the other great movies I listed above - *The Shining* stands out as my favorite horror film of all time.

With kicks and punches,
Xoxo, Hollywood

THE EVIL DEAD

BY BRIAN NETTO

Writer/Producer/Director
Delivery: The Beast Within, Intruders,
50 States of Fear: Grey Cloud Island
Twitter: @TypeABfilms Instagram: @Nettworxx

Favorite horror movie? That's easy. Sam Raimi's *The Evil Dead*. Hands down, without question, seven days a week and twice on Sunday. But here's the funny thing; as I re-watched the cult classic in preparation for this piece, I began to realize that Raimi's brutal, 1981 debut feature wasn't quite the film I remembered from my youth. This was largely because so many of the moments that I thought belonged to *The Evil Dead* were actually from Raimi's 1987 follow up, *Evil Dead II*.

Over the years, both films had somehow melded into one singular movie in my mind – so much so, that I couldn't discern which line or moment or dismemberment came from which film. With *Evil Dead II*, Raimi had essentially re-imagined his own film before re-imaginings become all the rage in

Hollywood. And here's the thing – I love BOTH films equally! I couldn't choose which film to write about for this book, so I'll write about both: a gooey, Karo syrup-drenched love letter to both entries and, more importantly, to Raimi himself, whose fearlessness cemented him as THE most influential genre filmmaker of my childhood!

There's really nothing quite like discovering a film for the first time, particularly in the era in which I first watched *The Evil Dead*. It was on VHS, as it happens. Before Rotten Tomatoes. Before IMDb. Hell, before the internet. Snatching a film off the rental shelf was truly a leap of faith. All you had to go on was cover art, or the recommendation of fan magazines like *Film Threat*, or in rare instances, that ONE guy or gal working at the video store for whom this wasn't simply a minimum wage job, but rather a subsidized film education. Millennials, you'll never know the agony of showing up to Video Update (my video store of choice back in Woodbury, Minnesota) for one specific film only to find out it had already been checked out, because, chances are, they only had one copy. Believe me, for the films I liked, they never had more than one. It only helped whet the appetite for a movie even more knowing that I had to wait until my next visit.

My father had converted our basement into a man cave long before the term became popularized, and I often retreated there to watch these films. This particular film was something I had designated as a daytime viewing for obvious reasons. Look, our basement was big and dark, so don't judge me…

The Evil Dead was the very definition of a video nasty. It even had a quote from the Stephen King on the cover proclaiming the movie to be the scariest thing since…well, Stephen King. And from the first grainy frames, it did not disappoint.

It was lo-fi, sure, but that's what made the film so chilling and fun. It also inadvertently served as inspiration both to myself and my childhood friend and now co-writer/co-director, Adam Schindler, as it had that same DIY backyard film quality that we saw in our own early film efforts.

For the record, that designation is absolutely meant as a compliment, as it has nothing to do with the low budget and everything to do with the love and passion that was splattered all over the screen; you could see they were having the time of their lives making it and that this film wasn't a business decision, but a love letter to a genre they had a great affinity for. And it shows in every frame, every scene.

Horror has been a passion of mine for as long as I can remember. It's the reason we made a *Child's Play* ripoff homage as kids featuring a Cabbage Patch Kid. It's the reason I brought a knit glove with straightened paper clips taped to the fingers to my third grade class after I saw my first *A Nightmare on Elm Street* film. We pour that love for the genre into everything we create. After Adam and I began screening our first film *Delivery* at festivals across the country, we often heard from fellow filmmakers (non-genre filmmakers, I might add) that we were smart for making a horror film since "horror sells". We'd smile and correct them, letting them know this was no business decision – it was done out of pure love, pure passion. And it was easy to recognize in *The Evil Dead* (and every film Sam has made since, frankly) – it just looked like he was having FUN.

With *Evil Dead II*, Raimi had moved into something I like to call "Popcorn Horror." Sure, I'd laughed plenty while watching horror films before (often AT the film instead of WITH it) but *Evil Dead II* was the first time I can recall experiencing a film that encouraged laughter as much as it wanted you to jump out of your seat or feel the urge to empty your stomach from any number of the bloody gags. You may not have left the theater scared out of your mind but you certainly left on a movie high.

Headless corpses perform beautiful dance numbers in the moonlight. The woods themselves harass, chase and penetrate our main characters. Dismembered hands taunt their former owners. It was the sort of mayhem you didn't think would, could or should be committed to celluloid, and yet, Raimi brought a playfulness to the carnage that had you covering your eyes and laughing at the sheer audacity and inventiveness of it all.

"I'll swallow your soul."

I want to focus on that phrase, because that phrase, in my opinion, is what horror is all about. Horror is about those ideas, those images, and those scenarios that reside somewhere just outside the realm of the real. I had no earthly idea how one might go about swallowing a human soul and, honestly, I didn't want to find out. It sounded precisely like something that came from the mouth of the undead and thus, nothing I wanted any part of.

Raimi's cameras traveled through glass windows, swooped over bubbling marshes and leveled trees in pursuit of its prey. The unspeakable, unstoppable, unseen force tormenting our doomed characters was all the more devastating because its power knew no bounds. As for what it looked like? Well, that was left largely to our twisted little imaginations - something I had plenty of.

Recently, Adam and I had the good fortune of working with Sam on an upcoming horror anthology. I'm sure you've all heard the popular refrain to steer clear of meeting your idols because inevitably they'll disappoint you in some way, shape, or form, but for some reason I never feared that with Sam. Call it naiveté but for some reason he always struck me as "one of us", and by us, I mean a fan. And I'm happy to report that he's been every bit the genius and collaborator we could have hoped for.

Put a gun to my head, I'd probably have to go with the original as my favorite of the two but they're both great in my book. It's like choosing between regular M&M'S and Peanut M&M'S – both are delicious. It just depends on your mood.

THE PEOPLE UNDER THE STAIRS

BY

FRED TOPEL

Journalist

Rotten Tomatoes, Popdust,

We Live Entertainment, Monsters and Critics

Twitter @FranchiseFred Facebook: @FranchiseFredOfficial

For most of the '80s, I was too scared to watch horror films. In my defense, I was born in 1977. I had a friend who kept trying to get me to watch horror movies and told me the *Nightmare on Elm Street* movies were comedies. How could that be? Freddy kills people. That's not funny!

But in 1988, I let him show me the first three *Nightmares* and they captivated my imagination. Whether they were scary or not, they were about kids facing their fears and learning to use their own dreams to battle the ultimate nightmare. Yes, Freddy was funny, but I recognized his macabre humor didn't make it a comedy. Wes Craven became a name I admired. *Nightmare 4* was the first horror movie I saw in the theaters with that friend.

By 1991, I was interested in anything Craven was making. There was another Freddy movie out that year, purported to be *The Final Nightmare*. Fortunately it wasn't, but Craven outshone the franchise he created (and would soon return to with his *New Nightmare*) with his latest original, *The People Under the Stairs*.

Craven was probably the second filmmaker I ever knew by name. The first was Steven Spielberg, because his name was on all the movies as either director or producer that I watched as a kid. But Wes Craven's name was above the title. It was Wes Craven's *The People Under the Stairs*! I must have known who Scorsese was shortly after, since *Cape Fear* came out a month later. John Carpenter was a name like Craven, but I was on my way to discovering him.

Craven read a news story about a family who called the police to report a burglary. When the police arrived, they instead discovered that children were being abused and forbidden to go outside. That seed inspired an even more elaborate urban legend about that scary house the neighborhood kids are all afraid to go into.

Fool (Brandon Adams) is a kid whose family is going to be evicted. So he joins his sister Ruby's (Kelly Jo Minter) boyfriend Leroy (Ving Rhames) and Spencer (Jeremy Roberts) to rob the landlords (Wendie Robbie and Everett McGill). Inside the landlords' house, they find booby traps that prevent their escape, a terrified captive "daughter" Alice (A.J. Langer), and kidnapped children kept in the basement, under the stairs.

What hooked me was the house of booby traps. Secret compartments lead to new corridors for escape and trapdoors send villains back to the kitchen. The interior of this house must be three times as big as it is outside, but Craven always gives it a sense of geography. I think my fantasy was to venture into a house of horrors (like Jim Henson's *Labyrinth* as a house) and escape. My assumption was that I'd emerge triumphant on the other side. Spencer and Leroy weren't so lucky.

I think what appealed to me most was that the heroes were

kids. At 13, Fool and Alice are even younger than the *Nightmare* teenagers. And Roach (Sean Whalen), an escaped person under the stairs, was still a young teenager depending on how long he's been living in the walls. Now the villain wasn't a monster, but just bad "parents." As a kid, parents can be the scariest monsters. I had great, generous, loving parents, but it's just the condition of being under their power that makes them scary. The idea of kids really striking back against abusive parents was really empowering. *The People Under the Stairs* was my Home Alone.

Even now that I'm officially a grown-up, I still relate to the kids rebelling against their parents. I guess you never outgrow feeling like a rebel standing up to oppressive authority. Mommy (Wendie Robie) and Daddy (Every McGill) do say familiar parental threats like, "If I have to come down there, you'll be sorry" or "You kids will be the death of me," even though what they're doing is far worse than any standard parental discipline.

I hope I could be as brave as Fool. He gets out first but he's not going to leave Alice there. He creates an elaborate scheme just to get back into this house of death to save her. He reports Mommy and Daddy for child abuse, knowing the cops will only go through the motions of checking out the house, but he uses that distraction to sneak back in. When Fool climbs out of the cabinet after the police leave, that is badass.

The People Under the Stairs also endeared itself to me with its slapstick sense of humor. Roach and Fool would really beat up on Daddy like he was Wile E. Coyote. Fool even uses the booby traps against the house, shocking the attack dog with the electrified doorknob. It was very *Evil Dead II*, which my horror neighbor also showed me. Even though at first I resisted the idea of horror movies as comedies, it turned out that I really do prefer my horror with some laughs. The idea of watching a movie about people getting killed is kind of absurd anyway, so you might as well have fun with it, but I also think it's an effective way to misdirect tension and give a false sense of security.

It was still scary though. Mommy and Daddy were relentless. Their traps and dogs jumped out of nowhere to frighten you. Roach is scary until you learn he's nice. There was plenty of gore too, but the most terrifying idea was the real world horror of kidnapping and child abuse. Human monsters could convince themselves they are righteous and commit these atrocities. That's scarier than monsters in masks.

Mommy and Daddy are magnificent horror villains too: she is *Mommy Dearest* turned up to 11, and he goes from snarling and dancing for joy to getting dazed by slingshots, bricks and crotch punches. (And he wears a gimp suit three years before *Pulp Fiction* - also starring Rhames - popularizing it, as he hunts the kids in the house.)

The older I got, my cultural sensitivity only deepened my appreciation for the film. This wasn't just kids striking back. This was an African-American kid leading the rebellion against the rich white landlords oppressing their tenants. There was a social commentary in the way the landlords called themselves Mommy and Daddy, the way Ronald and Nancy Reagan did. Even removing the Reagans from the equation, the late '80s/ early '90s superficial rallying cry of "family values" by politicians who did not embody any such real values was manifested as Mommy and Daddy, literally kidnapping children to make their perfect family and discarding the ones who disobeyed. When you learn the full backstory of Mommy and Daddy, their faith-based values are beyond hypocrisy.

When I became a journalist, I dreamed of getting to interview Wes Craven. I was lucky enough to land several interviews with him from 2000 to 2013. It was a lucrative time for him film-wise, directing *Red Eye* through *Scream 4* and producing remakes of *The Hills Have Eyes* and *Last House on the Left*. I first spoke to him at the launch party for the short-lived *Total Movie* magazine, and last promoting AMC's short-lived streaming service YEAH!, which offered *A Nightmare on Elm Street* with his commentary.

Every time I brought up *The People Under the Stairs* it seemed to make him happy. I'd list it among *Nightmare* and

Scream as influential favorites and he'd say, "I'm glad you have *The People Under the Stairs* in there." I think this one was personal to him and one he didn't get asked about as often. When I told him it was my favorite horror movie, he was surprised and said, "Really?", but graciously accepted my praise, "Oh, fantastic." He would tell me about building sets with portable walls in order to achieve the camera angles and giving his cinematographer grief by lighting dark corridors with only a match or lighter.

During a period where a reboot was considered, he speculated that maybe the freed kids had "gone off and built a magical kingdom someplace." I sort of think it would be worth exploring how those traumatized kids could reacclimate into society, but that wouldn't be a horror movie. No plans to remake *The People Under the Stairs* came to fruition, not even the TV series for Syfy. While I'm sure there is a modern interpretation of *The People Under the Stairs* worth telling, now that Craven is no longer with us to produce it, the original film will remain his definitive statement on people living under stairs, the 1% creeps who keep them there, and the young generation who can make things right.

DAWN OF THE DEAD (1978)

BY

KEVIN SHULMAN

Director/Writer/Producer
I Am Fear
Instagram: @KevShulman

Here she is…reigning since November 1978, and held over for now forty plus years, by not so much popular demand, but by cultural demand…the undisputed heavyweight champion of zombie films…she needs no introduction people. It's *DAWN OF THE DEAD.* The film's vision, execution, and cultural staying power is an axiom to all those that know this genre well. Disagree? *Return of the Living Dead*?? *The Beyond* you say? That's cute, but at some point someone in life needs to tell you you're a silly person who likes silly films. *Dawn* is anything but that! It's the magnum opus of the politically minded horror filmmaker, George Romero, whose genius redefined the genre.

Romero didn't invent the zombie film, he reinvented the zombie film. He put the brains into the zombie genre and created a sociopolitical sounding board, assuming that his audience had brains and weren't zombies themselves. *Dawn of the Dead* is a reflection of the American collective nightmare. The 1970s brought in the protracted end to the Vietnam War, a continuing Cold War building up to an Armageddon, and a stranglehold of Capitalistic mammonism preventing minorities from actualizing their American Dream. The zombies in this film play and live out their own desires and fantasies, just as the characters, Peter, Fran, Roger and Steven fight to maintain their personal sense of identity.

It was never in Romero's appetite to just scare the audience. His films also demanded that they think...setting him aside from even masterful filmmakers like Alfred Hitchcock, who strings his audience along like marionettes in a suspenseful puppetry. Hitchcock was a master manipulator. Romero, rather, challenges the intelligence of the audience with his tactics of portraying race reversal, class warfare, and jingoism. The film is a love letter to the political better nature of Americans; an atta boy saying, "I know you can see through this bullshit being shoved down our throats;" a call to action for the intelligent, not the rich, to govern this country and influence the rest of the world.

DEAD ALIVE
(AKA BRAINDEAD)
BY
SAM BOXLEITNER

Actor/Writer/Director/Composer
Downstairs, Die! Sitter! Die! : Rupert
Instagram: @SamBoxleitner Twitter: @ SpawnOfTRON
Youtube: @SonOfTRON

I have to admit that I was a bit nervous when I was first approached to write this. My favorite horror movie? That's a tough one. I remember embarrassing myself once while being interviewed by Michael Klug (a writer, actor, and aficionado of all things horror) when he asked me the same question. He grimaced after I replied with *Psycho*. "Oh, come on! You can do better than that!" he said. I still stand by that answer in a way. If I was to give an award for the greatest horror movie ever made, why not go with the mother of modern horror? But the question asked wasn't, "What's the greatest horror movie ever made?", the question was, "What is my favorite horror movie?"

In the coming days, I would reflect on what I love about the genre and the films that molded me into the filmmaker I am today; and more so, the filmmaker I strive to become. When I was a kid, every Friday night was "pizza and horror movie night." Friday night was by far my favorite night of the week. I will never forget the night we brought home *Braindead* (a.k.a *Dead Alive* here in the U.S.A.). I remember running to the kitchen and dry-heaving in the sink after watching a VERY infected Vera, or "Mum," squirt bloody puss into a man's pudding, then watch him happily eat it while complimenting the pudding's creamy texture. I can still hear my then seven-year-old brother, Lee Boxleitner, cackling in hysterics, sitting cross legged on the floor, as Mum's ear fell into her pudding and she proceeded to eat it. I had never been so horrified, disgusted, or amused by a movie before. If I remember correctly, we even taped over an old Betamax tape so we could continue to enjoy the film long after we'd returned the VHS tape to it's home at the video store. I probably watched it a hundred times. But it's going to take a lot more than nostalgia for me to claim a movie is my favorite. Allow me to go into why *Braindead* is my favorite horror movie of all time.

If comedy is tragedy dancing, then horror is all of that, but on acid. That's *Braindead* in a nutshell. *Braindead* is Peter Jackson's third film. You may know of him as the guy who did what many said was impossible and turned Tolkien's great epic, *The Lord of the Rings* into a multi-Oscar award-winning trilogy (in my opinion, one of the greatest achievements in film history). I was not surprised at all when these films turned out amazing. I'd seen Jackson's earlier work. I'd seen *Braindead.* Peter Jackson is a master at creating a world, no question. Using bright colors when most filmmakers would go dark, and using unorthodox lenses and camera movements that at times almost put the audience in the nostrils of the subjects they are watching. He is also a master of set up and payoff.

One of my favorite shots in *Braindead* is when the protagonist, Lionel, parks his lawnmower over the camera, showing the lawnmower blade slowly spin to a stop. For first-time viewers, they have no idea that this is a set up for the greatest example of a third act fun and games sequence in horror movie history. If you've seen this movie before, you know exactly what sequence I'm talking about. If you disagree with my assessment, FIGHT ME.

Whether or not *Braindead* is a SCARY movie is completely subjective. It may have gotten me a couple times during the first viewing, but it was through subsequent viewings that I began to fall in love with the film's other qualities. Braindead is not only beautifully shot, accompanied by a fantastically whimsical score, expertly performed, and rock-solidly written, but it is one of the goriest films ever made and flat out hysterical. One might even say that it's a comedy before calling it a horror movie. But let's make no mistake; *Braindead* IS a horror movie, through and through. Though I've always had a love for this movie, it wasn't until watching it again in preparation for writing this essay that I discovered *Braindead*'s true brilliance. Though the dual meaning within the film's title is somewhat obvious, I had never captured the true duality of the film itself. On the surface, *Braindead* is a comedically gruesome zombie outbreak flick. But beneath the surface, there is a sub-current theme that is eloquently told through its characters and beautiful camera work. Strangely, this theme has nothing to do with horror at all. Or does it?

Let's take a look at *Braindead* on its surface. The film follows Lionel, a man living with his mother Vera, who is chastised for his relationship with a Spanish corner store employee named Paquita. After secretly following Lionel and Paquita to their clandestine date at the zoo, Vera or "Mum" is bitten by a rabid rat-monkey, turns into a zombie, and slowly but surely converts a colorful cast of characters into an undead horde. It's up to Lionel and Paquita to take on the horde and save their town and possibly the world. Though the names have changed, this concept has been delivered a hundred times before. But it's the film's core theme that sets it aside from its counterparts.

(If you don't believe me, ask actor/writer Simon Pegg. He has openly said that *Braindead* was the inspiration for his zombie horror-comedy *Shawn of the Dead*, which contains the same core theme.) The theme in question explores us human beings and our struggle with growing up into well-adjusted adults. I could go through and give you a shot by shot breakdown of the film but I'm not going to. Trust me, the theme is there. In every shot, every scene, every sequence. What I would like to go through, is the film's colorful cast of characters. Not only are they incredibly fun, but they either represent us, or the obstacles and challenges that keep us from becoming fulfilled adults.

The characters I'd like to examine are Lionel (the protagonist), Paquita (the romantic sidekick), a nurse, a priest, a rebel, a demonic zombie love-child (the zombies in the basement), and finally, Vera, or "Mum" (the antagonist.)

Here we go...

Lionel: played by Timothy Balme, is FUCKING BRILLIANT in this role. His slapstick approach to the character is very reminiscent of Bruce Campbell's approach to Ash from the *Evil Dead* franchise. However, unlike Ash, who thinks he's a bad-ass, Lionel is the antithesis of machismo. He's actually kind of pathetic, which is sadly why I think I relate to him more. Though I would love to be able to come up with the perfect thing to say at the quintessential time, and inspire a legion of the living to stand up and fight an army of the dead, regretfully that is just not me. In reality, I'm a klutz, and at this point in my life have failed at every "great" venture I've set out to take on. Sure, I've had small victories here and there, but I assure you that I've lost far more battles than I've won. I sometimes wonder why my beautiful wife has retained such faith in me the way she has. I am devilishly handsome, so I guess I got that going for me...anyway, back to the subject at hand. Like all great protagonists, I see a piece of myself in Lionel. In a way, he is the filmmaker's reflection of me; and of you, if you're being honest with yourself. However, unlike most protagonists, Lionel doesn't seem to have any desires when we first meet him.

Lionel is the poster boy for Stockholm syndrome, kept from developing into a confident man by his mentally and emotionally abusive mother. He goes about his day, blindly obeying his mother's every command, appearing to be completely comfortable in doing so. Though easily in his twenties, he is constantly treated as a dopey little boy, and without even realizing it, plays the part willingly. It will take an act of fate for him to realize that not only does he have desires, he has a newfound necessity: the need to be FREE - more specifically, the need to be FREE TO GROW. Unfortunately, it's going to have to take facing a zombie horde in order to meet that need and blossom into the man he's meant to be.

Paquita: portrayed by the adorable Diana Peñalver, is the love interest in the film, but her part in the film's theme is far more important than just that. She is the physical embodiment of Lionel's need: FREEDOM. Though initially sheepish in her presence, Lionel slowly becomes more confident as he gets to know Paquita, until eventually, he is no longer a dopey boy when he's with her. He's a MAN, man! Unfortunately, this will be short lived, for like all of us, Lionel has a lot of psychological baggage with him that will get in the way of attaining what he desires.

Psychological baggage that is personified by the following characters...

Zombies in the basement: This is where things get a little weird. As the film progresses, Lionel subdues a group of zombies and locks them in his basement - all of which embody a different fear or obstacle that we face while becoming an adult. An allegory all in it's own, is it not? Let's take a moment to dissect the monsters in Lionel's basement...

The Nurse: or Nurse McTavish, played by Brenda Kendall. The Nurse represents money and security in our future and the fear of not having either. I'm sure many of you had dreams growing up. Maybe you're like me who had dreams of becoming a rock star who would segue into becoming a movie star/ filmmaker that would inevitably be chosen to help establish the first human colony on the moon. And every time you mentioned your dreams, you were told that most likely said dreams would never come true and that at the very least you should come up with a plan B. Maybe the conversation went like this -

DAD
So, kid. What is it you want to be when you grow up?

YOU
Well, Dad, I do really love to dance...

Dad
(beat)
You're going to be a doctor.

Or a nurse. Something stable. Something guaranteed to offer security in your life. And that thought will burrow into your brain and transform into a fear that will lay eggs that hatch into a million little baby fears. "What if my dreams of being the next Ginger Rogers are unrealistic?" "What if I'm not good enough? There is SO much competition in the dance world right now. How will I stand out? Dreams are great and all, but they might just put me on the street and I can't live like that because I absolutely NEED at least two baths a day. Maybe I should find a plan B..." But when that plan B requires at minimum eight years of higher education, internships, residencies, and so on, that plan B soon becomes your only plan. Scary shit, right? Let's not think about it right now. Stuff that fear somewhere deep down and stay a kid a little while longer.

The Priest: or Father McGruder, played by Stuart Devenie, represents our fears that we will inevitably fail at being righteous, good God fearing people. (Some of us were never "God fearing" but that's neither here nor there. You get the point.) When we are kids, we are innocent. But that doesn't last into adulthood and there is an inner fear in all of us that we will never be that innocent again. The truth is we won't. We may strive to be good people, and for the most part we are, but at some point we will fail at it. We are all destined to fuck up. A lot. "May he who is without sin cast the first stone." Not a lot of takers in THAT story. We are not perfect, we are all with sin and will eventually fail. In *Braindead*, there is an amazing scene where Father McGruder literally "Kicks ass for the Lord" and embarks on a truly epic kung fu battle with three rabid zombies. Unfortunately, despite his divine power he is bested by the beasts and becomes one of them. So, why grow up and try to be anything if we're just going fail regardless? Let's stay kids a little while longer.

The Rebel, or Void: (played by Jed Brophy, depicted as a rockabilly punk) symbolizes the party animal that we all have in us, no matter what age we are. Even Ol' Granny still needs her three o'clock brandy. Though our inner rebel helped some of us get through our college years, he's not the kind of guy you want to have around all the time as an adult. Sure, sometimes we'd all like to say, "Fuck it. Whuddya say we all drop what we're doing, go down to the cemetery, have five or six whiskeys, and let the evening culminate in pissing on tombstones?" Might sound like a good idea at the time, and the rebel inside would surely agree, and maybe, just maybe, if you were still a kid, it actually would be a good idea. Might learn something. But as an adult, this is NOT a good idea because the ramifications could lead to at the very least a bad headache and grass stains on your hundred dollar jeans. Worse, it could lead to a hefty fine or even jail time. Kiss all that hard work at making a secure future for yourself goodbye. Or better yet, stuff that rebel back into the dark hole you've kept him in and never let him out.

Demonic Zombie Love-child: or Selwyn (played by Morgan Rowe, Sean Hay, and voiced by Vicki Walker), symbolizes our inner child. Not that being in touch with our inner child is a bad thing, but I'm sure we've all known someone, maybe in their thirties or forties, who still spends just a little too much time playing video games instead of actively trying to pay their rent. Peter Jackson once recalled in an interview that one of his favorite scenes from the movie was the one where Lionel takes baby Selwyn to the park in an attempt to be the good father he never had. But Selwyn is a terror, possibly because he's a demonic zombie love-child, and wreaks havoc on the park. The park patrons don't see Selwyn as the problem though. He's a baby. Babies are innocent. All they see is Lionel's vain attempts at subduing baby Selwyn. He ends up leaving the park with Selwyn, stuffed into a bag, coming off as an abusive father; shamed.

This is symbolic of the shame that occurs when an adult is caught by the world around them over coddling their inner child. It could also be symbolic for one's fear of failing as a parent, which also works within the core theme. Either way you look at it, we should probably bury that shit down deep.

And finally, Vera, or "Mum": expertly performed by the late, great Elizabeth Moody. Mum is the first zombie to be locked up in Lionel's basement (and for good reason). Mum represents the greatest fear we all face during our seminal voyage into becoming adults: the fear of becoming our parents. Ugh, shit! I literally get shivers when I think of this one. Don't get me wrong, I love all six or seven of my parents/step parents/parental figures. They are fantastic people and I have a great relationship with all of them. But I didn't go through years of therapy because I was born broken. They broke me. I was the brunt of some of their greatest mistakes and I'll be damned if I'm going to repeat those mistakes. But it isn't that easy, is it? Shit doesn't just roll downhill. It snowballs down from generation to generation. Our parent's mistakes mold our psychology and it is nearly impossible to avoid carrying some of them with you. That is truly terrifying. I don't want to spoil the end of Braindead for you if you haven't seen it, but let's just say that Lionel's confrontation with his mother at the climax of the film is VERY symbolic. To a nauseating degree...

Let's start wrapping this up. Lionel tries desperately to keep his zombies locked up in his basement, hiding them from the world around him in order to protect the world AND himself. (After all, no one wants to be caught with five corpses in their basement! It just doesn't look good.) This is to his detriment because the more he is preoccupied with the zombies, the further and further he is drawn from Paquita - aka, his freedom. To make matters worse, the more he tranquilizes the zombies, the stronger they get. Despite Lionel's attempts at subduing the them, they eventually break out of the basement and infect an entire impromptu party of hepcat Kiwis (symbolizing everyone and everything around him). If Lionel would have simply just killed and buried his mother at the first sign of trouble, none of this would have happened. But he didn't, and now he has to face all of his troubles at once. I don't know if you can relate to that, but I sure as hell can.

In conclusion, I think what makes *Braindead* my favorite horror movie is that it is more than what it seems. 99% of horror movies only offer what is on the surface, and that's not always a bad thing. Sometimes, all I want is to watch a masked lunatic slaughter a bunch of half-naked camp counselors. Sometimes, all I need is a bunch of furry space critters to terrorize the farm. But sometimes, isn't it nice to get a little bit more?

Braindead not only presents a fantastically colorful, gruesome, and hysterical surface. It also offers a message that transcends the genre, like a horrific poem that says what it wants to say but means something so much more. As I write this, I am thirty (let's just say I'm in my thirties), have a wife and child of my own, and I still deal with the zombies in my basement. I've learned a little stress from the nurse isn't always a bad thing. Sometimes she's just the kick in the balls I need to get my shit together. I've come to peace with the priest because I know that I am a good person who will fuck up and it's alright. I'll make things better again. I always do. I've learned that the rebel is good in moderation, especially during a game of beer pong. And the demonic zombie love-child? Well, now that I have a child of my own, I've come to learn that in certain situations baby Selwyn can be my best friend in the world. As far as Mum is concerned, I've learned I am stronger now than my parents were BECAUSE of their mistakes, and my mistakes will make my child stronger than me. Evolution in all its wonders. But still, sometimes the zombies in the basement grow hungry for flesh...their appetites, insatiable. Sometimes, they cannot help but break out of their prison and infect our precious little worlds. What do we do in times like these? I say, we do what Lionel would do. Strap a fucking lawnmower to your chest and go to town on those festering, fiendish, little weeds. Sometimes a bloodbath is inevitable. Don't run from it. Dance in it. With a lawnmower. Strapped to your chest.

PHOTO BY: NICK HOLMES

LADY IN WHITE

BY
TIFFANY SHEPIS

Actor
Tales of Halloween, The Violent Kind, Victor Crowley, Deathcember
Twitter/Instagram: @TiffanyShepis

Coming up with a favorite among the many I've seen over the course of my life is massively hard. I went back and forth with the classics like *Rosemary's Baby* and *The Exorcist*, and then found myself reminiscing about the first time I saw *Fright Night* and the fun I had with local NY classic *Scream for Help*.

After giving it much thought, I had to go with the little known and rarely talked about kiddie horror/fantasy *Lady in White*. One reason is, I'm sure this is NOT on anybody else's list but also because, as a child, it scared the living shit out of me.

Lady in White is not gory. It's not graphic. It's not fun, but dark, unsettling, and heavy.

A little boy (Lukas Haas) gets locked in his classroom coat closet overnight by total asshole bullies on Halloween. While he's trapped in the closet, he sees the scene of a little girl getting murdered. The little girl is a ghost and fucking terrifying. First of all, being locked inside anything is terrifying, but imagine being locked in your classroom closet on Halloween in upstate NY? Upstate NY is creepy AF on it's own!

Anyway, the kid (Haas) is now on a mission to help the little ghost girl find her killer. There's some mad creepy imagery and to this day a song that gives me the chills, "Did You Ever See a Dream Walking?" Let's also not forget the very beautiful and very creepy Katherine Helmond as The Lady.

Lady in White didn't have any real impact on my life or career, but it did have a hand in solidifying the fact that I wanted so desperately to make movies that were scary or strange or unsettling.

Lady in White is by no means a horrifying movie that will stop you from sleeping. But having watched this as a child and feeling like I could be that little girl murdered in a coat closet, it somehow resonated with me to this day. It's not often that movies without spectacular graphics or amazing plotlines can follow you 20-plus years, but this one has. I dare you to watch that little girl dance around singing that song and not be creeped the fuck out!!

So yeah, yeah. *Chainsaw* is scary as hell. *A Nightmare on Elm Street* (Tina in body bag, OMFG) and *The Exorcist* are terrifying. *Jaws* too...But, did you ever see a dream walking? Well, I did...It's called *Lady in White*, and to this day it makes my skin crawl.

PHOTO BY: JOSH KATZ

THE TEXAS CHAIN SAW MASSACRE
(1974)
BY
BRIAN HENDERSON

Podcast Host/Photographic Artist
Forever Midnight Podcast
The Keepsake Remains, Night Drive
Instagram: @ForeverMidnight_Podcast
Instagram: @Phantomacabre_

Visiting my cousins was always a treat growing up. One cousin was a few years older than me and the other was my age. I didn't get to see them more than once or twice a year but when we'd go to visit, it was usually for a few days at a time. That time together was consumed with trying to impress each other and making bad decisions about fireworks - specifically, how close you should set them off next to fingers and faces. I always looked up to my older cousin, mainly because he was into all the stuff I wanted to be into: heavy metal, punk rock, rap music and of course, horror movies. Being younger, I was far less informed than he was, and to make matters worse, I was unable to find out about a lot of it because of my age and lack of money. My older cousin turned me on to so many things that, even now, at 43 years old, I am still into.

One particular visit when I turned 12 would change my life forever. This time started out like they all did, mostly running around outside, throwing firecrackers at each other and walking to the local mini-mart for candy and Cokes. At the time, VHS rentals were popping off, and since my cousin was the oldest, he picked what we would be watching that fateful evening. To set the scene, my Aunt had a daycare she ran out of her home for many years, so my cousins had a bunch of additional random kids that had become like little brothers and sisters running around their house. Inevitably, as olders sibling, we torment the younger ones. I don't know why, but it's in our DNA. My older cousin absolutely loved tormenting the younger kids at the day care, and when we younger cousins came around, the youngest - my little brother - caught most of the heat. The oldest cousin loved to try and scare us, and was happiest when someone ended up crying. I'll admit that - in trying to impress him - I did all I could to torture my little brother as well.

That fateful night, we were going to eat pizza and watch some videos that my Aunt was picking up at the request of my oldest cousin. He didn't care what we wanted to watch, he loved horror movies and loved the fact that they would make us all whimper in a corner. At least, he hoped for that reaction. He had heard about a super messed-up movie with a name to send shivers up your spine: *The Texas Chain Saw Massacre.* Even I had heard of this movie, though I was just starting to dip my toes into the world of spooky, scary movies. It was notoriously the scariest, goriest horror film you could get your hands on.

I was terrified and at the same time so excited to watch this nightmare unfold right before my eyes. My brother was not at all interested, and I would even say, hated anything that could be considered dark or scary. On Halloween for instance, I would always be a bloody ghost or Frankenstein, while he would dress up as Bugs Bunny. Watching horror movies that night was the last way he would have wanted to spend the evening, but we older assholes made it a rite of passage and insisted that we ALL watch. Don't get me wrong, I already liked monsters and aliens, but even I was very scared to face this movie head on. We gathered around the TV and pushed play on the old top-loading VCR. I still remember how I felt as I was about to witness what was surely going to be a snuff film. It all felt so raw, so real, and I (like everyone who has ever seen this little low-budget horror film) somehow saw so much more blood and gore than there ever actually was on screen. I sat frozen, cross-legged on the carpet, too close to the screen, but I didn't dare scoot back so as not to show fear in front of my older cousin. So, I just watched. My mouth hung wide open, and I was unable to believe the horror I was witnessing.

When the dust cleared and the credits rolled, I was finally able to ingest what just happened. For the first time in an hour and twenty-three minutes, I remembered my poor younger brother. He also sat on the floor crossed-legged, closer to the couch - and he was on the verge of tears. He hated every minute of that movie. He was so completely bummed, and the perfect time to torture him further would have been right then - but I couldn't, as my own mind was blown. I couldn't stop thinking about this movie. The colors, the locations, the dread. How real it all felt. I had no idea about how movies were made, and as far as I was concerned the events I saw had all actually happened. I mean, I knew it wasn't real, but I couldn't believe that a movie could make me feel this way.

I was instantly hooked. From then on, I could not get enough blood and guts in my life. I bought every *Fangoria* I could and I watched every horror film that I could get my hands on. Later in life, when I started to take my own photographs, I focused on themes of death, murder and gore. I realized that the whole idea of how I wanted my photos to look and feel all came from this dirty little horror movie that some film students pooped out one hot summer in 1973. Years later, after talking about horror films nonstop, I now get to co-host a horror movie podcast where I reference *The Texas Chain Saw Massacre* every seven to eight minutes. To this day, it is my absolute favorite horror film and I believe it still stands the test of time. For me, as long as I am creating art and photography, or just talking about what I love about horror, I will always look at this film as a template for how I want people to think and feel while digesting my own work. It has totally and completely influenced how I want my photography to look: gritty, bloody, raw, and filled with dread.

TRAIN TO BUSAN
(AKA BUSANHAENG)
BY
JAY KAY

Collector of Conversations/Festival Programmer
A Strange Man in a Film Land
Horror Happens Radio, HorrorHound Magazine, Dread Central, Horrible Imaginings Film Fest
Twitter: @HorrorHappensRS & @FestTravelerJK3
Instagram: @a_strange_man_in_a_film_land

This essay took me nearly the entire deadline to fully realize, organize, and finally write. For this book, I considered writing about movies such as *The Strangers*, *Night of the Living Dead*, *Deathproof*, *Audition*, and *The Ninth Gate*. All these films have a personal connection to me, but in different ways. For weeks and weeks, I could not put the pieces together. I challenged and confronted myself with what story or lesson or moment would be attached to the selected film and how I could present the impact it had on me. As I sat across from one of the greatest people who I have ever known and love so much, it came to me. Decompressing from the frustration at the formica table, it became clearer as I talked to my fiancé. It was going to be *Train to Busan*. It had a personal connection to me that was about love and experience. A film that sparked my love of wanting to be part of film festivals and to make dreams happen even after I turned 40. So, let me tell you about a film, two festivals, and a friend on one Sunday afternoon in Montreal.

For a good five years now, I have been extremely immersed in horror film festivals. Most years, I attend about 20 festivals on average to experience, collect conversations, make memories, and see horror through other filmmaker's eyes. Back in 2016, I made the choice to attend one of the largest genre festivals in North America. It was my first year there and the 20th year overall for the Montreal-based festival odyssey known as Fantasia. For those who do not know, Fantasia is a three week celebration, curated by some of the most respected voices in the industry presenting incredible programming and events. It usually showcases well over a hundred features, tons of shorts, special events, guests, and so much more. Many genre names of today and yesterday take to the stage in a celebration of dreams and nightmares that come true in front of the rabid Fantasia audience. So many films have come through those doors of the SGWU Alumni Auditorium over the past twenty years and leave with a stamp of respect by the Fantasia faithful, no matter how their film was received. If you have gone before, you know what I am speaking about. If you have not, get there! The energy of the festival, the beauty of the town, and the passion of the attendees makes it a must for film fans. It fuels me each year.

In my early stages of festival coverage and attendance, I had known and interviewed the talented Hugues Barbier from his East Coast-based film festival called the Ithaca Fantastik. He's a man of great taste in genre film and an inspiration to me on many levels. Ithaca was an eclectic and eye-fluttering exploration into cinema. But I digress. That first visit to Fantasia was overwhelming. The first couple days I attended, I was lucky to bump into plenty of the names who I've had conversations with on my horror talk radio program, *Horror Happens Radio*. Back then however, I dealt with some anxiety. And well, Fantasia is a bit overwhelming no matter how many festivals you attend. During the three weeks, the festival takes you in so many different directions, whether it is making the choice of what films to watch or getting around town or getting to know the community, it's a lot to take in.

Getting back to Hugues, if it had not been for him, I am not sure I would have made it through. See, in my life experience, I believe that we all have a plan that we are following. As we move through life, we meet people along the way that help us through and direct us. Nothing is by chance and everyone you meet is meant to serve a purpose as part of that plan. For me, if I had not bumped into Hugues that morning of the screening, I don't believe I would have seen this movie. Things are all connected.

That Sunday morning in 2016, I was one of the lucky ones, however, to be at the screening for *Train to Busan* in the main theater. Walking in with Hugues, we sat center to the screen and off the floor waiting to see what was to unfold from this hyped movie that had so much buzz coming out of Cannes. For me, I knew that Fantasia always featured some of the best films from the Asian film markets from countries like Japan, Korea, and more. It seemed that, not only did this feature have much anticipation, but many of those who moved the gears of indie horror made it a point to attend the screening on a Sunday. Anyone who comes to Fantasia knows that a lot of drinking, laughing, and talking happens every night. This makes early screenings a bit tough. For me though, the anticipation of the film built a buzz in my chest. I have loved Asian genre cinema for years, and it has played an important role in getting me through some bad times before. Sitting down in the seat, listening to the introduction, and experiencing the interaction of the audience, it had every element of something brilliant and memorable! As the film unfolded before us, *Train to Busan* did something that was lost on most genre cinema, it gave us something to care about amongst the chaos and horror.

Train to Busan is one of the best examples of the undead sub-genre in the history of horror movies. Created by animator Sang-ho Yeon, the film blends the action of his background, the troupes of the sub-genre, and a humanity which makes it special like *28 Days Later* (and a majority of the Romero catalog). Yeon succeeds in pacing the film by understanding how to drive this story rollercoaster (or in this case the bullet train). Humorous interactions and comedy beats are placed well and snapped off by a clever little girl and a brave, muscled man (god love Dong-seok Ma/Don Lee). *Train to Busan* has a lead protagonist and lead antagonist, who deal with guilt as reflections of what could be and what is. It has the scariest villains possible for me. Simply, they are us...the infected and the very alive, panicked masses. The film is a survival story primarily on a train, presenting themes within the narrative that only horror could do without a backlash.

Sitting there with Hugues in the auditorium, the energy of the packed crowd was so powerful. We were living the emotion, horror, and tension during the run time, moving through that train with each character, connecting to their conflict and story arc. We were shocked and gut-punched. We laughed, cried, and we talked back to the screen. For me though, this was not the sole set of reasons why I chose this film for my essay. No, this film has impacted me so much more since that screening.

Before I get to that, the next time I saw this film was in October at the Toronto After Dark Film Festival. Up to this point, I'd seen *Train to Busan* three times on the big screen (and was continually blown away each time I watched it). The TADFF screening stands out because of one scene that may be my favorite ever in a genre film. (For those who have not seen *Train to Busan*, please watch it as soon as you are done reading this essay and take in the pure power and passion of something special! For those who have seen it, you know what I am talking about.) The scene revolves around the lead trio of characters in an empty train car: the businessman father, the muscled father to be, and the teen baseball player going into hell, who each have a loved one trapped several train cars down with only one way through the fast and nasty undead masses. As the trio figures out how to make it through while getting suited up with padding, baseball bats, a shield, and their will to survive, the scene plays out like riding on a roller coaster nearing the top and suddenly letting you fall. Now, in many undead films, the protagonists confront the undead masses with guns or tanks or some sort of weapons. Not in *Train to Busan*. This is another reason why it's my favorite horror movie. The film's director, Yeon, decides to send Dong-seok Ma's character "Sang-hwa" into the undead conflict, with just his taped fists and a focus to rescue his wife and unborn child. No room to run or hide. No way, but through.

As the trio enters the train car full of the infected, Young-gyu Jang's score raises and the train door slides open. Sang-hwa goes right into the masses using his power and speed to destroy them as the father and teenager use their weapons to move into the next car and the next challenge. The way the battle is shot in such a closed area is so tense, fluid, and clever, utilizing the sound, emotion, score, and the unfolding of the action with various horror elements. It's as perfect a scene as you will ever find in a horror film. After watching that scene at Fantasia, the crowd was spent, but we roared with cheers. It was unlike anything I had ever seen and or ever experienced in a theater.

Train to Busan, not only created a viewing experience that I would never forget, but it became one of my favorite horror movies from that moment forward. Now, what about TADFF? Well, after Fantasia, all I could do was talk about the film to others. It had left an impact with me from that experience was just starting its festival run. I attended TADFF during that year and I was lucky enough to be there when it screened. Sitting in one of the large theaters at the Cineplex Scotiabank, I decided to sit front and center again for the screening. It was as great as the first time, with powerful sound and stunning picture that recreated a magic all over again. I relived all the moments from that film and even roared when the score rose and they entered the car with taped fists, a shield, a club, a bat, and the humanity to survive.

Going forward, I realized that this film and that experience gave me that boost to keep going to festivals. It helped me build confidence and continue to grow what I had in my head. It opened so many doors, took me to so many places so far, and helped me to create so many friendships along the way. *Train to Busan* created characters, emotions, and conflicts you could connect to, which was key to the love I have for it. That is the macabre beauty of horror: human at the core and unrelenting. Many films forget that we need to connect to both the protagonist and antagonist, because we are both: a man who wants to save his daughter; a father-to-be wanting to save his wife; a pair of sisters; a crowd panicked and dangerous; a human monster, who wants to see his mom one last time; a guy like me, who finds a calling and comfort in film festivals, being able to follow his dreams. That is the magic of *Train to Busan* and that is why it is my favorite horror movie.

A NIGHTMARE ON ELM STREET
(1984)
BY
CHRIS SERGI

Producer/Development Executive
*I'm Just F*cking With You, Monster In My Family*
Instagram: @Chris.Sergi Facebook/Twitter: @ChrisSergi

What can I say about my favorite horror movie, other than it completely changed and influenced the trajectory of my life, only to come full circle.

Let's start at the beginning. When I was a kid, I was the biggest pussy (not much has changed, but in my head, I'm Floyd Mayweather). Anyway, I was a little runt of a kid. I was afraid of anything remotely scary, especially when "fake." Plastic and rubber spiders, dinosaurs, snakes and little paratrooper men terrified me. So, when I needed to go on playdates, my mother had to call ahead and let my friends' parents know to keep them hidden so I wouldn't freak out.

My mother had enough of these shenanigans, so she decided I needed to learn about the magic of SFX. How did she do this? By putting me in a room to watch the *Thriller* VHS over and over again with the behind-the-scenes footage of how they executed the practical SFX. It seemed to really make an impression on me, and after that, my fear turned to curiosity. I was in first grade at that point, and we somehow thought it would be a good idea to watch *A Nightmare on Elm Street*. It was still pretty new to home video, so there was no movie theater involved.

When Tina was dragged up the wall and ceiling by Freddy, that was "the" moment. It clicked with me. I got it. It's fake. It's fun. I want more! As my mother would continue to introduce me to things like Stephen King (her favorite author of all time), *The Exorcist*, and more classic gems, my obsession for the genre grew and would eventually be the driving force in my career. As I grew up, the release of horror movies became pivotal events for me to look forward to. I could never wait until the actual release date.

But Freddy was my favorite. Years later, as I came into my twenties and had a pretty steady career position, but I became bored and uninspired. I loved work and loved to have consistency. I was making great money for someone my age and had been living independently since my late teens. In about 2006, I had enough. I was going stir crazy and need to try something else. I saw my life being so predictable. I worked at the same place doing the same thing for the same hours per week. But what could I do? I was a high school dropout, who, after getting my GED, went to community college only to drop out. I was great at business and climbing the ladder, but I'd move up till there was no place left to go. I was tired of hitting my head on the ceiling. I wanted to love what I was doing, and I wanted a legacy. What could I do for work where universities wouldn't dictate how far I could go and how high? The entertainment industry. There are no rules. The industry is always changing, and people maneuver that industry with all types of backgrounds. I gave notice, packed up, and drove cross country from Boston to LA. My goal was always to make movies that I'd want to see. I've made and worked on all types of projects over the years, but the goal was to be a "name" in the genre and have a livable career executing these projects with people I enjoyed being around. Now, 13 years later, the majority of the work I've done in the last two years has been in the horror genre. How this all comes full circle is, a few years ago, while developing a TV project, I got connected to Heather Langenkamp. Since then, Heather has become such a dear friend of mine who is always supportive and helpful in any way that she can. My most recent completed feature, stars Heather Langenkamp in the cast...so to come full circle all these years later is really kind of mindblowing.

I was watching *Nightmare* this past weekend and it's still scary. It still holds up as an iconic movie that will always hold an important place in genre history. It changed my life. It changed the lives of those people involved in the production and the fans new and old who discovered it...and I think it's safe to say, in these unsettling times, we can all learn a thing or two from Nancy Thompson.

THE EVIL DEAD

BY
THERESA TILLY

Actress
The Evil Dead, Oz the Great and the Powerful, The Stomping Ground
Facebook: @Ladies.of.Evil.Dead Twitter: @TheresaTilly

I have been asked about my favorite horror movies a few times. But, much like the anxiety I have in watching horror movies, I've dreaded discussing them. It reveals too much about my own psychological peculiarity. But mostly it exposes my simplistic understanding of them. So I always deflect, saying, "*The Evil Dead* of course, I'm in it!" However this time, in order to express myself with sincerity and fulfill my obligation to this brilliant compendium, I've tried to be less glib and to reply with confidence and honesty. This required a couple afternoons of re-watching scary movies and it was actually, FUN.

What made *The Shining* so terrifying for me, even the second time, was that it seemed so familiar. Shelly Duvall's large trusting eyes and the motherly way she acted toward sweet little Danny instantly took me into the story. A more adorable child could not have been cast for the trusting Danny, who also changes his cute little boy voice to play his friend Tony, who advises him while he lives in his mouth and uses his index finger to speak. I sympathized with all the characters, even Jack, who seemed cruel enough to be somewhat abusive. But I didn't think he was really dangerous until he took the job at the Overlook Hotel. The killer in him was stirred by the isolation of his situation. I get it, a waning lack of inspiration, and a recovering alcoholic without an AA meeting nearby, some things are just too much to bear.

It seemed like a good idea to work there at first, the hotel was beautiful and majestic in the snowy mountains, yet its remoteness seemed more taunting than the kind of solitude that a writer might need for creative inspiration. When I take long road trips through sleepy towns and imagine my life in those distant homes on hillsides, I often think I'd love to live there. No one is around but nature.

A remote haunted getaway, voices that are believable but possessed, normal people in unusual circumstances, all remind me of one of *The Evil Dead*'s themes. On just a normal day with normal people, things can go very wrong. The two movies also have inappropriate humor in common when Jack axes down the bathroom door yelling, "Honey, I'm home" (a familiar conversation under the circumstances); similarly, *The Evil Dead*'s "We can't leave Shelly, she's our friend" after Scotty and Ash have hacked her to pieces and are debating how to bury them - I mean her. In the end, it's the fight to survive that gets me. Wendy and Danny make it out and Jack is frozen in the maze. There are a few obvious loose ends, but it's such a wild trip, I just don't care.

Poor Norman Bates. He was clearly browbeaten by a bulldog of a single mother. And then when he finally grew up and killed her, liberating himself, he couldn't live without her. Sadly, it explains a few boyfriends. You just don't get a lot of matricide movies, so I found it scintillating to explore those motives.

The isolated and vacant Bates Motel ("where the highway used to be") provides another example of how it might be best to room in a more populated area, a Motel 6 near an all-night bar maybe. I don't know if Sam Raimi is a Hitchcock fan, though after making *Evil Dead* he did start wearing a suit every day to film, in homage to Hitchcock perhaps.

Another similarity is the strange angles and shots they both used in their respective openings. The first stuttering view of Psycho's Phoenix, Arizona, then sudden close up of the room where Janet Leigh and boyfriend are finishing up a little afternoon delight reminds me of that shaky-cam zooming and bumping through the swampy woods in the opening moments of *ED*.

I couldn't help but make the comparison of *Psycho*'s choreographed stabbing in the shower to Shelly pulling back a shower curtain in *The Evil Dead*'s first possession as she attacks Scotty with blade like fingernails. I prefer the implied stabbing and blood of Hitchcock's shower scene, and if it were up to me, all horror movies would be so discreet.

After seeing *Scream* I understand why Sam Raimi refused to discuss our acting motivation with us as we often requested. He just told us exactly how to move and didn't care if it made any sense to us. I thought *Scream* had that element to it, too. No one cares why you say it, they just want to see it happen. I was sucked into the thriller aspect of who was murdering these kids; it had to be someone they knew. That suspense aspect of it kept me engaged.

I felt like I was unraveling a cold case with the found old news footage in *The Texas Chain Saw Massacre*. Five kids on the way to a concert really reminded me a lot of *The Evil Dead* (five kids on their way to a cabin), except the *TCM* kids were the way cooler Jessica Biel version of us. Their relationship to each other was also very similar, only we were more Midwestern and polite; I really loved the make-out scene in the back seat while the front seat people watch in the mirror. I loved seeing the moral fiber of Biel's character as she fought for each ridiculous character's life. The love and attraction she and her boyfriend had was very sexy. I think, of all the scary movies I've ever seen, the Leatherface character turning around with Kemper's face sewn on him was the scariest moment ever. Of course the chainsaw business, now that really brings back a lot of fond *Evil Dead* memories.

Surprisingly, a few years ago I decided to go see a horror movie in the theater. And believe it or not, it was my favorite movie for the entire year. *Get Out* made me laugh out loud - a lot. The humor was so unexpected and the commentary on our society was brilliant. I almost selected it as my absolute all-time favorite.

However, for today, my favorite horror movie will remain *The Evil Dead*. I'm in it after all, but after seeing it so many times, I think all the simple scares and kooky stunts still get me. I love that the actors are taking it all so seriously as the director all the while is grinning in his beer. Blend this with great music by Joe LoDuca and make-up and effects handmade by Tom Sullivan. And when you compare that budget to anything else, it's somewhat incredible. I like to look at it from the female point of view, three badass possessed women kicking the butts of the jerky men in their lives, it just doesn't get more modern than that. I'm still too scared to watch *The Hills Have Eyes*. Maybe next time.

EVENT HORIZON

BY

DYLAN MATLOCK

Producer, Writer

Along Came the Devil, Captured, Ouija House

Instagram: @MatlockFilms Twitter: @TheDylanMatlock

Picking a favorite horror movie is a difficult task for me; my tastes continue to evolve. In my mind, *Alien* stands out, successfully straddling horror and science fiction, and driven forward relentlessly by the suspense engendered in the hunter/hunted theme. I loved the world created in *A Nightmare on Elm Street*; exploring the blurred line between reality and the dream state always intrigues me. *Shaun of the Dead* effectively blended comedy and horror with a tight script that paid off handsomely in just 100 minutes. These films continue to influence my work in the genre.

But two films really scared me when I was young and have always stayed with me because of it. The first was *The Never-Ending Story*. The relentless, existential force known as "The Nothing", along with the wolf creature (Gmork) haunted my thoughts, but I was fascinated and had to watch it over and over again, wearing down our VHS tape in the process. The idea that all we have to combat oblivion in our shared imagination (and storytelling) truly stuck with me.

The second movie that truly frightened me, and the one I want to talk about, was another film all about staring into the abyss. That movie is *Event Horizon*.

Although I was still too young to experience it in its full glory on the big screen, my brother and I picked it out in our weekly stop at the local Blockbuster. I remember watching it with my family in the relative safety of our basement screening room and its images were frightening for sure (a calmly aflame man with melting skin; numerous impaled and maggot-ridden corpses; evil Sam Neill). They shocked and scared each and everyone of us. To this day, I recall a lot of gasping and covering of the eyes, all amid a continuous faint whimper that I initially mistook for background ambience intended by the sound director. I think my little sister is still hiding amidst the dropped popcorn behind the convertible couch we lounged on during our family fun nights. At the time, I shared a room with my brother. Neither of us could sleep, staying up all night talking about the movie. And the next night. And the night after.

Event Horizon touched on some interesting themes and also used its setting to such great effect. I find that a lot of these themes pop up in my own work today.

First, the setting. There are few things more unnerving than isolation. And what's more metaphorical than a spaceship adrift in the vast emptiness of space. From the moment the crew boards the *Event Horizon* (a mysteriously re-appearing ghost ship they've been sent to explore), there is this feeling of being alone.

Their own ship, the *Lewis and Clark*, is aptly named for a sense of pioneer spirit. Them wanting to see if there is an end, a place that's further than anything known. *The Event Horizon* itself was made for such a purpose. Exploring that desire to try and comprehend the nothingness at the end of an ever expanding universe.

The crew is tight-knit, almost a family. The young engineer, Justin, even has the nickname "Baby Bear" and he calls the middle-aged medical tech, Peters, "Mama Bear". Laurence Fishburne is the ultimate patriarch, worried only about his crew and less about the "mission".

Family also plays a big part in the crew's nightmares. The failure to be able to save the ones you love is what haunts them the most. *Event Horizon* exploits these anxieties and turns the ship into a living hell. Peters (Kathleen Quinlan) is tortured that she lost her son to a disease she couldn't stop. Captain Miller's (Laurence Fishburne) regret is having to make a hard decision that cost one of his crew members, his family, their life.

Dr. Weir (Sam Neill) regrets abandoning his wife; an act that led her to take her own life to avoid the loneliness of an existence without him. The image of her eyeless face as she beckons him to join her was probably the image that stuck with me the most. Terrified and conflicted in pondering which path to choose, his desire to return to their bliss - unachievable as that is - drives the final act.

The movie also touches on the limits of perception: the notion that we perceive only with our physical senses. Dr. Weir tries to breach the limits of the universe; to experience a concept we have no way of experiencing. In the end, he removes his eyes, knowing that they are useless in the next voyage.

The production design aligns perfectly with the director's vision. The ship is less a realistic space vessel than a gothic cathedral. I remember the shadowy corners and the striking contrast with a crucifix window. There is an infinitely long dark corridor that leads to the gateway room, a giant sphere with rotating rings and lights guards the gateway (itself a black pool, like an evil Stargate), the meat grinder blades that circle around the walkway, and of course, the cramped crawl space, lit with nothing but green lights. All of these images create a sense of danger, but it also makes the *Event Horizon* feel like a beautiful tomb.

Though certainly a flawed film, *Event Horizon* provoked other questions a young watcher wanted answered, thoughts that I shared with my brother for many nights after watching it. The theme of a family unit trying to deal with oblivion or up against a force that's hard to comprehend is something I've tried to include in my own work. For this reason, it still resonates with me all these years later.

FRIDAY THE 13TH PART 2

BY
EBEN MCGARR

Founder/Writer/Director
Mad Monster, Sick Girl, House of the Wolf Man, Hanukkah
Instagram: @MadMonstergram Twitter: @MadMonsterMag
MadMonster.com

I can never pin down any favorite film, let alone subgenres like horror films. If I considered *The Exorcist* a horror film, MAYBE that would be it, but I don't. However, thanks to an ambiguous title in the heading of the guidelines for this project (referred to at the time of this entry as UNTITLED MY FAVORITE HORROR MOVIE SEQUEL), I interpreted it to mean we were discussing our favorite "horror movie sequel." That, for me, is easy, so I'm hijacking this essay to share with you *Friday the 13th Part 2*, my favorite horror movie SEQUEL (even though I know damned well before starting that it's not what is being asked).

Friday the 13th Part 2 has everything I want in a slasher film. It's *The Godfather: Part II* of horror. It arguably has my favorite horror score by the great Harry Manfredini, one of my all-time favorite slasher casts, and a top-notch script so ahead of its time. Tom McBride's portrayal of wheelchair-bound Mark is not a sympathetic character to be pitied but a strong, charismatic, cool kid who dies as brutally and memorably as anyone else. That was inclusion and representation before it was reduced to a trendy hashtag. Then there's Jason. No longer just the tragic cautionary tale of counselor negligence from the first film, this is really the first appearance of the most iconic screen killer of all time. Before his trademark hockey mask, with that unsettling bag with one eyehole cut out, adult Jason is back for revenge after seeing his mother killed. His story has come full circle, and they basically redefine the franchise here while keeping the same style and tone that worked so well in the first entry. Seeing that disturbing shrine with Pamela Voorhees' head surrounded by candles, and the fact that the cop was so close to catching him (in a great daylight chase scene I always appreciated), there was a sense of realism. It was a time before cell phones, before the internet age, when urban legends about wild men so far off the grid were still plausible.

I loved this franchise so much, I hosted the NecroComicon 25th anniversary celebration of *Friday the 13th,* May (Friday the) 13th-15th 2005 in Hollywood, CA. I invited Cliff Cudney who was the stunt coordinator for Part 2 and was pitching to him how great it was going to be. Everyone was attending... Sean Cunningham, Betsy Palmer, Corey Feldman (in his first horror con appearance), Nick Savage (in his first and what was possibly his only convention appearance), and dozens of others like Warrington Gillette who played Jason in *Part 2*...Cliff cut me off. "Who played Jason in *Part 2*?" I was confused, how did the stunt coordinator not know this? Warrington was on the horror convention circuit for years, EVERYONE knows who he is. I figured I'd refresh Cliff's memory...turns out his memory was fine. "You're looking for Steve Dash." I frantically searched on the internet, IMDB only showed Warrington at the time, there was no mention of Steve ANYWHERE. Then

Cliff explained in great detail a story that is now infamous. He gave me Steve's number (they had kept in touch and Steve was a taxi driver at the time). I called him and he simply couldn't believe anyone cared about "some dumb movie" he did over 20 years ago. I assure him we REALLY REALLY do. I then make the mistake of explaining how successful Warrington is at the show, thinking that it would demonstrate how successful Steve would also be. Instead, it enrages him and he interprets it as Warrington stealing credit for his work. This story is well-known now. They both showed up to my 25th anniversary show and Steve went after Warrington hard, shouting across the show floor. He sounded like Tony Clifton as he repeatedly screamed "I'm the real guy...that guy's a phony!" Sean Clark met him at that show and interviewed him in a piece that ran on *Dread Central*, breaking the story for all of the horror community to hear. Sean would go on to rep Steve, and fans across the country got to meet him and let him know just how we all appreciated his work.

To me, one of the greatest gifts to horror fans is *Friday the 13th: The Game*. It nails the atmosphere of the films and you get to play as Jason portrayed by Kane Hodder! Kane is my favorite Jason, but appears in my least favorite films of the franchise. Seeing him nail every performance from Baghead to *Jason Lives* solidified my belief that he IS the definitive Jason. Watching him do Brooker's run...so good. My company, Mad Monster, basically pioneered the celebrity costume photo op. I am the one who spent hours on the phone with Kane convincing him to do *The New Blood* photo op in Chicago the first time after showing him how good all our previous ops looked. I assured him we would have Buechler recreate it and it would be amazing. It was. Well, after playing the game, I wanted to take it to the next level and have him do a Baghead Jason photo op. He was adamant that he wouldn't do it because he "didn't play Baghead." I argued that he played Baghead more extensively than either Warrington OR Steve in that motion capture. He had already agreed to do the exclusive 8-bit and Savini Jason photo ops for us (which I pointed out never appeared on film, yet were as significant as his Baghead portrayal) and, so, my all-time favorite sequel, with my all-time favorite Jason became one of my all-time favorite photo ops.

Note that it was not a greenscreen photo op. We built a full 1:1 replica shack, the photographer was hidden and the photo op was taken candidly. The photo op experience included an immersive walk-through set with DEE WALLACE portraying Pamela Voorhees and FELISSA ROSE and DERON MILLER playing promiscuous counselors. Yes, Angela was there too!

SCREAM

BY GUS KRIEGER

Writer/Director/Producer
The Binding, Fender Bender,
Would You Rather, The Killing Room
Twitter: @MrGusK

In the winter of 1997, myself and about a half-dozen of my comparably-aged extended family members gathered in my parents' upstairs bedroom, shut the door, dimmed the lights, and popped in a rented VHS of Wes Craven's modern meta sleeper phenomenon *Scream*.

Highlights of the night included but were not limited to the following: I played it cool in front of my adolescent peers, acting as though I'd already seen the movie in theaters (I hadn't), half the group became fixated on trying to guess the identity of the killer out loud (they didn't), and my younger sister was rendered a scarred and blubbering mound of nerve endings who would not shake the trauma entirely until college (when she saw *The Strangers* and kickstarted the cycle all over again).

The experience also cemented my personal leap into a full-fledged adoration of horror films which, up until that point, had never been more than a burgeoning infatuation.

I've asked myself in the intervening years what it precisely was that made this happen, and the fact of it seems to boil down to one unifying admission: I'd simply been unaware that a movie could do the things *Scream* did. Drew Barrymore, by far the single most famous cast member and largest face on the poster, dead within the first twelve minutes. The main characters? Uniform geeks, hyper-literate and enviably well-versed in genre film, always ready with a snappy observation or incisive catchphrase (or sometimes both at once). The tone? Terrifying one moment, laugh-out-loud funny the next. "The Rules?" Good gravy, the characters in a scary movie are talking about how to survive a scary movie! The killer? There were two killers! Was all that even allowed? Who let this happen?

It was enough to turn my neophyte cinephile brain positively inside-out.

In less-skilled hands, Kevin Williamson's revelatory screenplay would have become little more than a self-referencing spoof. Luckily, ensuring this would never be the case was one Mr. Wes Craven, who trained his professorial eye on the many high concepts at play and anchored them firmly within a world always recognizable as our own (with the possible exception of a rickety garage door leveraging lethal force against a hundred-plus-pound human being). The respective sensibilities of screenwriter and director were thus ideally matched: adrenaline-fueled set pieces were balanced with carefully-calibrated tension-building, rat-a-tat dialogue with lengthy tracking shots, dark humor with sunny locations, irrational evil with mundane surroundings, wit with grit. It's a film that unfolds both deceptively straightforwardly and relentlessly present-tense, even as its audience is fed a slow IV-drip of information about everything up to and including its broken but resilient heroine, Sydney Prescott.

Much has been said about Neve Campbell's deservedly

star-making turn as both a prototypical final girl and strong female character, but Sydney is so much more. One quickly comes to understand that this is a person longing for nothing more than normalcy, a way out of the darkness and a means of putting her trauma behind her, even as said trauma begins literally manifesting itself to pursue her through the increasingly unlikely territories of darkened houses, high school corridors, and ladies' restrooms. This improbable pursuit, however, is entirely internally consistent; as the prologue and poor departed Casey Becker have made so abundantly clear, no one anywhere in this world is safe.

At Neve's side is a veritable medley of almost laughably qualified performers, many of whom would go on to headline feature films in their own right. Indeed, every rewatch offers new surprises with regards to who was showcased here first: Rose McGowan! David Arquette! Matthew Lillard! Jamie Kennedy! And, although the vast ensemble repeatedly proves more than capable, everyone down to the legitimate cameos like Henry Winkler - well after The Fonz but well before *The Waterboy*, *Arrested Development*, or *Barry* - and tiny throwaway roles are given impressive Coen Brothers-esque moments to shine: Sydney's teacher with one melancholy bit of dialogue, Casey's parents obviously discussing the flowerbed along their front walkway, Wes Craven himself in a brilliant walk-on ("Not you, Fred"). Though it must be said that Casting Director Lisa Beach's most baffling magic trick remains plucking generational all-star Liev Schreiber from New York stage obscurity for a nearly nonverbal passing glance of a role, thankfully ensuring his involvement in installments *2* and *3*.

Scream is also a structural outlier in the greatest possible sense. Many slasher films believe their best chance of maintaining audience interest lies in doling out a string of evenly paced and often increasingly elaborate kills, but *Scream* subverts the inclination entirely; in fact, a full fifty (that's five-zero) minutes pass between the first onscreen death and the second (RIP, Mr. Cousineau). The following kill occurs around one hour seven, and from there it's more or less a sprint to the finish line. Although the lesson of such structuring might seem thuddingly obvious, it bears repeating: we've spent over an hour getting to know this brilliant young collective, and there is now a fair amount of actual investment on the table once we realize only a select handful will be making it out alive. And caring about who lives and who dies results in an abundance of (imagine!) genuine tension, as opposed to a more traditional, disconnected experience based in rooting for the next interchangeable teenager to "get it."

Actually, have audiences ever rooted in favor of a slasher film's beautiful young people as hard as for those in *Scream*? The phenomenon occurs in no small part because the viewer is gently but firmly led to identify with them, with their knowledge and intelligence, even as they become overwhelmed by their extraordinary, horrific circumstances. It's all too easy to see ourselves in Sydney, pointing out that the typical horror heroine "is always running up the stairs when she should be running out the front door," before being forced by panic, adrenaline, and physical geography to do that very thing herself. Same goes for the character of Randy, sprawled on the couch and frustratedly bellowing, "Look behind you, Jamie!" at the television's playback of *Halloween* while he is himself obliviously stalked by the real killer from behind (the providential fact that *Scream*'s Randy and *Halloween*'s Laurie Strode are both played by thespians named Jamie is yet another of the film's minor meta miracles). In an additional fun bait-and-switch, audiences even come to identify with the initially grating tabloid journalist Gale Weathers (Courtney Cox, veritable veteran of the crowd, already post-Ace Ventura and mid-Friends), who emerges from the finale an unlikely heroine twice over, complete with a rousing one-liner: "Guess I remembered the safety that time, you bastard."

Such fist-pumping moments of "Hasta La Vista" excellence only work as well as they do, however, because of the patient slow-burns that have preceded them: David Arquette, for example, as the endearingly in-over-his-head Deputy Dewey, methodically making his way through Matthew Lillard's empty house as the diegetic soundtrack of *Halloween* melds with Marco Beltrami's omnipresent score; Rose McGowan's plucky Tatum caught helplessly halfway through the doggie door, bare legs flailing behind her; the silent rise of the hatchback as Sydney sits in the vehicle's front seat, horrifyingly unaware that the killer can now reach her unimpeded; the sweet triumph of Sydney's eventual victory would be nothing without these and many other distressingly sour sequences preceding it.

Williamson and Craven would go on to collaborate (to both varying degrees and levels of success) on *Scream 2*, *Scream 3*, and *Scream 4*. While all have flashes and even stretches of evident brilliance (as well as neatly inverting the typical horror franchise formula by maintaining its trilogy of stars and switching out its villains), the succinct perfection and nearly-plausible small-town satire of Number One would be born, live a rich full life, and conclusively end within those first one hundred and eleven minutes, severed as definitively by the blackness of its closing credits as one of its own fictional victims, falling prey beneath Ghostface's knife.

When said credits rolled across the screen of my parents' tiny tube television that fateful late-nineties night, several things had changed. One, of course, was the sleep cycle of my unfortunate younger sister. The other would prove harder to gauge but substantially more affirmative: I now officially loved scary movies, and would devote a considerable portion of my future to their consumption, analyses, and creation. Here was a genre that did not permit one's mind to wander, that would not tolerate your sitting in the dark making grocery lists or puzzling over which route you might take home. This was a category of entertainment with the sole aim of wrapping its sinewy hands around your neck, sinking its fangs in deep, and never letting go, 'til death do you part. And now I was part of the club.

Thank you Kevin, thank you Wes, thank you *Scream*.

PHOTO BY: JOSH KATZ

POLTERGEIST (1982)

BY
JEF OVERN

Horror Podcast Host, Artist, Musician
Forever Midnight
ForeverMidnight.net, ForeverMidnight.store,
Instagram: @ForeverMidnight_Podcast
Twitter: @FM_Podcast Facebook: @4verMidnight

Maybe it was the fact that I was around Carol Anne's age when I first saw *Poltergeist*, or perhaps it was because the film so brilliantly taps into basic childhood fears. You know the ones: monsters in the closet, creepy dolls coming to life, getting lost or separated from our parents, and the big one, a developing understanding of the unavoidable permanence of death.

To this day I still haven't really experienced genuine fear from any horror movie like I had when watching *Poltergeist* for the first time, and - get this - after countless viewings through my life it still holds up. That's no accident. First, we have two masters of horror at the helm, Steven Spielberg and Tobe Hooper. Each of these guys had already changed the landscape of horror in completely different ways with *Jaws* and *Texas Chainsaw Massacre*, so it shouldn't have surprised anyone that this movie would raise the bar. But I knew none of that, I was just a kid watching a movie that starts off light, easing me in, establishing a warm, recognizable reality. The trap had been set.

Poltergeist takes place in a familiar neighborhood. The house: similar to the one I was living in; a family that could have been my own. I was seeing my life reflected back at me, I understood the situation and felt right at home. "Home"...the one place you were supposed to be safe and protected. That's one reason why this little ghost story is so deeply disturbing to me: it revealed that I wasn't safe anywhere. My parents couldn't always protect me. I was a little kid staring at a TV late at night, watching another kid like myself staring at a TV when everything changed for her, evil things far beyond her control. I felt this movie was about me, I was experiencing everything with this family because, to me, they were my family.

The fear induced by *Poltergeist* was real, and it ran deep. This movie beautifully takes its time setting up The Freelings so can you feel this way. By the time the scares start you know who these characters are, you recognize this as an everyday reality. The ghosts aren't in some far off castle or an old haunted abandoned cabin in the woods. This was normal everyday life and an average American family. Then everything changes, and this normalcy that is so familiar and natural gets pulled apart like a rotisserie chicken.

When it comes to scares, *Poltergeist* pulls no punches. Spielberg and Hooper go so much further here than any other haunted house movie prior or since. You can present me a list of great haunted house films and each will lack something, some spark that is nearly indefinable. *Poltergeist* has IT: that secret ingredient the similar films lack. You can call it heart, intelligence, taking the subject matter seriously; call it what you will, but your contender for the throne is likely missing that spice, or it's been overpowered by other elements to appease the studios' broken concept of that horror fans want.

This is a film that doesn't waste its time on some convoluted murder mystery that our hero needs to solve in order for the spirits to rest like damn near every horror movie involving a ghost. It tackles the subject of losing a loved one and the big question of what comes after death without even one character dying! In fact, there is so little of what people usually associate with a horror movie, like blood, gore, nudity, etc. and it carries a PG rating! I bet no other horror film in this book will be able to stake that claim. In fact, its PG rating is likely why I was able to watch this movie at such a young age. "It couldn't be that scary, it's PG!" Wrong! It's all that scary! The suggestion of terror ALWAYS works better than a close examination of it. Too much information and it becomes clinical, too little and it's a WTF - hitting it just right is a masterstroke that can't fail. Suggest the scary thing, show me a bit, enough to fire off all those lovely chemicals in my brain, and move on. Remember in *Signs* when we saw that alien in the cornfield? Remember how all that tension was undone when they were crawling around on the roof waiting to get hit with the garden hose? I rest my case.

But I digress, in horror there is a time to throw the cards on the table and put something on the screen that will pay off the suggestion. When it was time to SHOW the scary stuff, Industrial Light & Magic created groundbreaking special effects that fully revealed things that only other movies could hint at, things from your worst nightmares. Horrific things happening to real people, people like you or me. That's horror. I see something terrible happen and immediately feel as if this is a situation I could find myself in, when the hypothetical starts to feel more and more possible.

This movie is the gold standard to which I judge all other horror movies, and it's an impossibly high bar to set. *Poltergeist* manages to be completely different than what came before it, yet still manages to be accessible and oddly familiar. *Poltergeist* is so well done that you forget you're watching a movie and lose yourself in it. This transcends genre and is the very essence of the form, but done in a way only horror can. Every filmmaker worth a damn wants you to forget that you are staring at a screen and get pulled into it like the late Heather O'Rourke.

At the end of this film I was changed. I had seen my fears personified, reflected back at me. I understood the finite nature of life. I knew that movies, not just any movies, but horror movies can do something more than just entertain, they can cause a physical reaction from deep inside you. They are capable of stirring up real emotions that touch the core of your being. Horror movies touch the very thing that has allowed our species to exist through the millennia, the thing that keeps us safe from harm, the feeling we have to confront if we are to do anything worth a damn.

Fear.

This movie defined me. After that fateful viewing, I was a horror fan through and through. Maybe it's a perverse addiction to the rush of neural activity, maybe it's being able to see life and death played out and still be able to walk away laughing with friends, hell maybe it's the popcorn...but horror is my passion, and *Poltergeist* was a critical piece to that revelation.

CARRIE (1976)

BY MARK CHAVEZ

Artist
Disco Bloodbath Art
Facebook/Instagram: @DiscoBloodbathArt

An awkward and shy high school student with telekinetic powers is bullied by her classmates for being an outcast with an overly zealous religious mother forcing her to live life as a good Christian girl. From director Brian DePalma's poetic opening sequence of *Carrie*, the film utilizes perfect cinematography and score to give us a feeling of innocence as our hero has her first period in front of all of her peers. The scene quickly descends into the hellish world of Carrie White: a world of constant bullying and harassment for simply being naïve to the real world around her. Somehow, she musters up the courage to face her fears and try to blend in for one night at the senior prom. Unbeknownst to her, some of the bullies have one last trick up their sleeves: to pick on Carrie one last time by rigging the prom ballots so Carrie and the handsome

Tommy can win Prom Night King and Queen and, at the exact moment, dump a bucket of blood on her. They would have the last laugh, or would they?

I first saw this film on television and I was 8 years old, my cousin Teresa, who was 16, begged me to watch it with her, but not to tell my parents. She promised I would love it and that the ending would leave me breathless. I was terrified. I had never seen a horror movie before. I was only 8 years old and raised by very religious Pentecostal parents. My cousin was babysitting us on the night of the television premiere and was so excited to tell us that she had seen the film with her family at a Brownsville, Texas drive-in. Her excitement was all I needed to give me the courage to face my fears to sit and watch a horror movie for the first time.

That night, I remember being quite nervous, but excited at the same time. After all, it was on television. How scary could it be? Turns out it was damn near terrifying, and mostly for personal reasons. In many ways, I WAS Carrie White, only in the body of a misunderstood and awkward boy. The ending not only left me horrified, but it ignited my interest in horror movies. The next day, I walked to the library after school just to borrow a copy of the book authored by Stephen King. You see, most of the movie was very biographical and personal for me. A lot of what Carrie went through, I was going through myself. I was bullied constantly. I had things like "eat shit" said to me, not to mention that my mother at the time looked a lot like Piper Laurie (who played Carrie's mother Margaret White). My cousin Teresa had a very strong resemblance to Susan Snell (played by Amy Irving), who was the only bully in the film to grow a conscience and make up for what she and the other girls did to Carrie by talking her boyfriend, Tommy Ross (played by William Katt), into inviting Carrie to the prom instead of her. She would rather sit the night out behind the curtains, trying her best shot at making a wrong a right.

Growing up in Texas with overly religious Pentecostal parents put me in a very awkward position with other students at my elementary school. Although I had a friend here and there, I was mostly an outcast due to the way my parents tried to raise me: to believe in what they believed even if it meant being bullied everyday. Even if it meant I was prohibited from watching anything outside what they considered "Christian" or "Godly." I was not allowed to go to any birthday parties unless it was someone from our church. I knew Carrie White, I felt what she went through, and although I never had a bucket of blood dropped on me (thank God), I experienced what it felt like to be odd, bullied for being different, and misunderstood. The prom scene felt like something I would love to have done to so many kids at my school. I lived vicariously through Carrie White. How satisfying would it have been to get revenge on the bullies? How nice would it have been to stand up to them and turn the tables? *Carrie* was a movie that affected me in many aspects because she was so relatable to me. So much so, that as soon as I returned the book to the library, I secretly went to buy a copy behind my father's back with my $10 monthly allowance. I eventually bought the soundtrack, only to have my father discover it (along with my *Fangoria Magazines*) and rip everything to shreds. It pissed me off and fueled my fire to go against the grain and take a chance, even if it meant dealing with the wrath of others. Years later, I still watch *Carrie* and it feels like yesterday. The power of that movie and that beautifully haunting soundtrack take me right back there where it all started.

It made me find solace in horror movies: an escape. I collected every horror movie advertisement in the Sunday Paper. I rented every horror movie that my local video store carried. I fell in love with the artistry, special effects, movie posters and VHS box art; I loved it all. I went to horror movie conventions like Monsterpalooza in 2016 and was blown away by all of the art, artists, and fans. Suddenly, I was with a lot of other Carrie Whites. Horror movie fans feel like family to me. It felt like I finally fit in somewhere, so much so, that I started doing my own art and am now a working artist who specializes in Horror Movie 3D Art. I followed my dream, something my father would have hated…Thank God.

EVIL DEAD II

BY CHRIS LORUSSO

Editor/Producer

How To Get Away With Murder, Hi-8, Portraits, Hi-Death, Kalamity, Cinemability: The Art of Inclusion

When I was asked to write this, I sorta went into a horror coma...how the hell could I pick just one out of the blood soaked plethora of beloved horror movies? My brain meats filled up with horror loves - *The Thing, Dawn of the Dead*, The *Shining, Dead Alive, Brotherhood of Satan, The Phantom of the Paradise, The Beyond, Gwar: Phallus in Wonderland, Mad Monster Party* - the list goes on and on and on. The sheer panic of this decision shot my anxiety through the roof. These movies came rushing at me and, like a deer in headlights, I stared frozen in my love for all of them. I spent a month pitting each movie against the other in a battle royale for the championship belt of My Favorite Horror Movie.

Then an axe cleaved into my thick skull...what horror film has most inspired, influenced, and been a part of my being since the day I saw it? The answer: *Evil Dead 2: Dead By Dawn*. From the moment I laid eyes on it I was pulled into to its gory, chainsaw-wielding, Three Stooges-loving grip, and it never let me go. As a kid, I'd sneak out of my room late at night and creep down to the living room to watch horror films on TV. We had a black box; for you younger readers, it was a descrambler so you could view all the encrypted pay channels for free, like a WWII code breaker for the cinephile. Thanks to this glorious device, I watched a lotta movies I wasn't allowed to see. I was 11, flipping through the cable channels, and a little, grimy, bloodsoaked, handmade movie was just starting. I was immediately sucked into its vortex. The reverse smoke. The VO that opens the film with "Legend has it that it was written by the dark ones" as the Necronomicon flies right at you and its stop motion animated flesh-bound face seemingly eats us as we are pulled into its evil hell portal full of spirits and demons; this is the film preparing us for the ride we're about to have (and what a ride it will be). After the end credits rolled off, I felt like someone had pulled out all my childhood obsessions - *Looney Toons*, *The Three Stooges*, monsters, stop-motion animation, video games, and presented them to me on a delicious, blood-splattered platter like I'd never seen before.

The film is chock full of great quotable lines: "I'll swallow your soul! I'll swallow your soul!", "That's right...who's laughing now...Who's laughing now!" and probably the most famous line from the film, and would come to be the one word that has defined Bruce Campbell's career, "Groovy." Campbell reprises his role as Ash Williams, which feels equal parts Robert McKimson's Daffy Duck, Larry Fine, and Steve Reeves' ultra macho Hercules. His craft shines in the largely wordless (other than screams, shrieks, grunts, and guffaws) first quarter of *Evil Dead II* as Ash deals with the demonic presence in the cabin by himself. Once we're brought up to speed on Ash's plight, the faceless demonic presence (or evil force) attacks him, and we get our first taste of the true hyperrealistic style of this film. Shot at what looks like 18 fps, Bruce Campbell is strapped crucifixion-style to what is dubbed the 'Sam-O-Cam,' which is just some plywood that holds down the actor as they rush him through the woods and other places. This early scene plays out like a low-fi cartoony version of the *2001: A Space Odyssey* star gate sequence, but this rebirth, while childlike, turns Ash into a horrifically-possessed version of himself. As he tries to regain sanity and break out of the possession, the sun rises, and we are given back our hero, slumped in a mud puddle. However this is just the beginning of the torture and humiliations our evil entity has in store for Ash. His dead girlfriend crawls out of her grave and does a creepy dance. Her severed head bites his hand. His hand gets infected with evil and he's forced to saw it off. And the entire cabin's inanimate objects laugh at him - even his reflection tells him that he's losing his fucking mind. All of this feels like a representation of what both Sam and Bruce were going through emotionally on the film they'd worked on just before, *Crimewave*, a small studio picture that seemed to go wrong every which way it could, and was finally taken away from them in the editing room. *The Evil Dead II* itself feels like its a personification of the studio that was coming down hard on Sam, Bruce, and Rob during *Crimewave* - the unrelenting evil never lets up, even when they think they've won, and Ash ends up sucked into a time portal to be lost in the past forever.

My favorite sequence occurs when the entire house laughs at Ash. At first, he tries to hunt down and kill his right hand after he cut it off and it ran into the cabin's walls. As he shoots at it, the cabin drips blood, and then, as if a pipe burst, the blood blasts out onto Ash and, just as suddenly, it stops. He knows he's losing it, sits down, and in a classic physical comedy move, the chair brakes, and Ash falls flat on his ass. Suddenly, a rotten deer head mounted on the wall turns and laughs at him. This leads to a crescendo of crazy, where the objects in the room all join in and laugh at him in unison. At first he's completely unnerved, but then joins in on the laughter, proclaiming in his actions that 'You can't break me!' This whole sequence might be one of the greatest metaphors for working in the film industry ever - if you can't roll with the batshit crazy things that may get thrown at you regardless of your role on the production, you won't survive. I feel this is a statement from Sam telling Embassy Pictures that they couldn't break him no matter how hard they tried. I've thought of this scene many, many times during the plethora of projects I've worked on and it still resonates.

This film is an early effort from KNB Effects, doing some incredible practical effects work on a limited budget. The possessed Henrietta bodysuit, the demon Ed mask (and subsequent hacking him up), the tree sequence, and the evil force being turned into a giant flesh face are all great and illustrate how this team was bound for bigger budgets and projects. In an earlier scene, after Ash saws off his hand, he gears up for battle, and in doing so, he attaches the chainsaw to his stump, creating the memorable chainsaw arm! This is one of the greatest moments in horror - the use of the chainsaw, while inspired by *The Texas Chain Saw Massacre*, deviates slightly in its conception. Instead of being a terror inducing weapon, it becomes Ash's Excalibur.

Evil Dead II was a huge part of what lead to me becoming an editor. I would set up my *Star Wars* action figures and take Polaroids of them, attempting to make rudimentary flip books, but being seven years old, they never worked out well. *Evil Dead II* was directed for the edit, and was cut like a big, bloody, live action cartoon. While I know this isn't the first time this was ever done, it's the first time it ever really struck me. I needed to understand how these moments played, such as the Ash preparing-for-war sequence where we heard his now famous line 'Groovy.' The shots and the timing of the cuts, blended with the hyper realistic sound design, all converged together for what felt like a seamless quick succession of shots that sped our pulse and prepared us for what was to come. The whole film is filled with these moments, wherein it felt Sam was directing it with the sound effects in his head. I love taking raw footage and putting those pieces together to build something organic that just plays, where the viewer doesn't feel the cut unless it's intended.

The first time I saw this film, it subconsciously implanted in me a love of film editing which has grown over the years. This film and a handful of others were the ones that pushed me into my career, and I've been very lucky that I've been able to make an okay living out of it.

The more I dug into the making of the film, the more wonderful it was to learn how the core team making it were old friends that started out making short films together in high school. They weren't film schoolers, or huge scholars - just fans of movies that went after it and built a new piece of the horror landscape, which took from their love of old horror and comedy but, molded it into a hybrid of something new. It's truly a wonderful picture, one that I don't know where I'd be without its influence in my life. If you're one of the few folks that hasn't experienced it, I implore you to borrow it from a friend, rent it, buy it, or see it at a midnight screening. You will not be disappointed.

If Sam, Bruce, Rob, Ted, or anyone else involved in the film ever reads this, all I can say is thank you. This film has inspired me in so many ways and helped a young weird kid find his path in life.

CHILD'S PLAY (1988)

BY
SARAH FRENCH

Actress

Blind, Rootwood, Automation, Art of the Dead, Desert Moon

Instagram: @SarahFrenchOnline

Twitter: @Scarlet_Salem Facebook: @SarahFayeFrench

I grew up in the small farm community of Melrose, Minnesota. At the time, the population was around 2,000. It was one of those communities where everyone knows each other. We went to the same church, same grocery stores, had picnics in the nearby park, and most worked at the big (and only) factory in town…including my mom.

I was raised in a single parent household with my sister Jessica. My mom had to work as much as she could in order to raise two little girls on her own. It was a struggle, but we managed. I turned out okay I think, ha-ha! Luckily, my grandma was around to help babysit us when my mom would be at work. We lived right across the street from the Lutheran church we would go to every Sunday. My mom would make sure we attended every week no matter what. As a kid of course, we never wanted to go but we had to. It was just one of those requirements when you grow up in a town like that. We could never get out of it, no matter how much we whined...although I did enjoy the treats they fed us and getting to play with our friends after the service.

Back in my day, we had video stores. Crazy right? Yes, I grew up in the era of VHS and video stores and I'm damned proud to say it. There was no better feeling to walk into a video store and go through all the movie titles, look at the covers, and pick movies based on those cool covers. It was such a different experience in the '80s and '90s with media compared to how it is now.

At the time, Melrose didn't have a regular freestanding video store. But luckily for us, there was one in the grocery store. We would visit the video store area, then get some groceries afterwards. We would have to rent a VHS player with it because they were too expensive for us to buy. It was always a sad day when we'd find plenty of tapes to rent but they were all out of players. Thinking back, it's kind of weird. Imagine going to Redbox and renting a movie and a Blu-ray player. Madness.

One day my sister and I went in the video store with our grandma to get some fresh new movies to watch. We would always start in the new release section. If nothing caught our interest, we'd move onto the classics we already loved. It's amazing that everyone now has access to pretty much any movie they want to see. My collection now is bigger than that damned grocery video store.

On this day, there was no need to move onto the classics. My sister and I saw the box for a movie called *Child's Play*. It intrigued us right away and we knew we had to watch it! My mom was always against us watching scary movies and would never let us rent any. So, as kids of course, when your parents tell you "no" on something, you want it even more. Luckily, we were with our grandma this time and could get away with a little more if we played our cards right. We showed the VHS to our grandma and gave her some story about how it's a kid's movie, etc. I'm not sure how it went down exactly, but looking back, she had to have known, ha ha! There's nothing kid friendly about it. But we were in farm country. The older generation tended to live in their own world and didn't realize movies like this existed. In many areas, they still do. So, she rented it for us.

I was around six years old when I first watched *Child's Play.* I was also six when I watched it a second, third, fourth and fifth time. We pretty much had it playing on a loop while we rented it. It is one of the very first horror films I can remember watching. From that day on, it completely changed my life.

I was so frightened of my dolls. I had to hide them until I knew for sure they weren't going to come after me to steal my soul. It was terrifying. With that being said, I loved the feeling so much, I wanted more and more! From then on, all I wanted to watch were horror films. It's still my go-to genre. Fuck romantic comedies. Give me some scares and boobs.

Child's Play holds a very special place in my heart because it inspired my love for horror. I can't tell you how many times I've seen it over the years, but it's a lot! Ha ha! I also immersed myself in the series (with *Child's Play 2* closely rivaling my love for the original). While other kids were watching Disney, I was watching Romero, Carpenter and Craven. I couldn't get enough. Without realizing it, I'm sure a part of the attraction of *Child's Play* was that Andy Barclay was my age. He was also growing up in a single parent environment, just like me. His mom was trying hard to give her son a good life and everything he wanted. As a kid, you don't really think about that. While reflecting on it later in life, it becomes apparent. I had quite a bit in common with Andy (other than, you know, a serial killer possessed doll trying to "Ade Due Damballa" the fuck out of me). I've been drawn to doll-based horror movies ever since, though none have quite reached the heights set by Chucky. (I do love *Dolly Dearest* and *Dolls* quite a bit though.)

When I became a teenager, I moved to the suburbs of the Twin Cities and met new friends that were into horror like me.

Now, I didn't have to feel like an outcast and hide my obsession. That's the thing about living in a small community: finding people that share your interests is tough. In a way, my friends were all the monsters that I watched. They were there for me no matter what. It was my secret obsession. To risk sharing it, would risk being labeled a weirdo. I've come to embrace that title though. I'm weird and there's nothing wrong with that.

My new friends and I would make short horror movies together. I would act in them and help create a script and film them on a camcorder. It was just something to do for fun. I never imagined being able to make real movies. We also played Magic: the Gathering together. I'm a proud nerd, through and through.

It wasn't until I was modeling in my early twenties that I began to think about acting as a career. I was going to school for criminal justice and close to getting my degree. I realized that it wasn't my passion. I didn't want to spend my life doing something I wasn't 100% in love with. I wanted to be that girl in a horror film running through the woods, half naked, covered in blood, fighting some sort of killer...or to be the killer. In 2006, I auditioned for a part in a short horror film called, *You're Next 3: Pajama Party Massacre*. The audition was just a meetup at a small coffee shop with the director and producer. They cast me that same day. Soon after, we were off and shooting. I got to live out my life-long dream of being in a horror film…and to this day, I'm still at it! Though I've yet to work on a killer doll movie, I hear there's a Chucky series in the works. That would be one of my dream gigs.

Over the years, I've been able to meet and work with some of my favorite horror icons. As a horror fan first and foremost, it's a dream come true for me. I've also had the pleasure of attending conventions and meeting so many great people, many of which, I now count as friends.

It's been especially amazing to get to meet the cast of *Child's Play*. The characters they played meant so much to me growing up. Alex Vincent, Chris Sarandon, Brad Dourif, and

Catherine Hicks, thank you so much for helping me discover one of the great loves of my life. I'm not sure how different my world would be had my Grandma not allowed us to rent the "family friendly" movie about a doll, but I'm damned glad she did.

H.P. LOVECRAFT'S RE-ANIMATOR

BY

JESSE MERLIN

Actor/Singer

Re-Animator: The Musical, Beyond the Gates, Bliss, Marianne

Instagram: @Jesse_Merlin Twitter: @JesseMerlin

JesseMerlin.com

Witnessing the rampaging severed head of a divided Dr. Hill in Stuart Gordon's monumental *Re-Animator* was a profound moment for this budding horror fanatic. Other films consumed me at a younger age, but nothing else had quite the lasting, indelible impact. After having my mind broken open and reanimated while a freshman at NYU, I became a devotee and attended midnight screenings whenever possible.

Imagine my surprise at being invited to audition for the role of Herbert West in Stuart Gordon's *Re-Animator: The Musical* while it was undergoing a workshop process at the Steve Allen Theater. Meeting Stuart was a terrifying thrill, but I felt properly prepared, having memorized a fair amount of music and dialogue for the audition. Not getting cast was understandably more crushing than normal. Little could I suspect that Graham Skipper, soon to become my eternal nemesis, was simply born to play Herbert West and take on the mantle of the title character, becoming a worthy successor to Jeffrey Combs' stupendous performance in the film. At the time, it was a bitter blow.

And then, a bolt from the blue: the role of Dr. Hill opened up six months later when the show was mere days from staging rehearsals and they needed to cast Carl in a hurry. Determined not to let another chance to work with titanic horror figure Stuart Gordon slip from my cadaverous fingers, I looked for inspiration to the tale of Peter Sellers' big on-camera break. First rejected for a character role in film, he went to the same audition a second time well-disguised in full age makeup, wig and costume. This time, he was cast on the spot. Knowing my youthful countenance would play against me, I tried the same angle. I'd had a modest career in regional opera singing my share of aged buffo roles, devils, generals, and grandfathers, so playing older was a specialty. Yet in the horror genre I was a complete unknown and felt compelled to make a strong sell for my casting as the bad doctor, especially since the theater was intimate, bordering on tiny.

The gamble paid off.

Re-Animator: The Musical opened the warm, sticky world of horror to me, and I've never looked back. No better place exists for outsiders and misfits of every stripe to come together and create.

Central to the enduring power of *Re-Animator* is a style common to Stuart Gordon films. He doesn't just take you by the throat, he reaches into your guts, twists, and makes you lean forward, never back. There's hardly a moment to catch your breath. His characters are complete people who care deeply and want real things very badly. Everyone plays to win. The villain is always on a twisted hero's journey of his own. David Gale's immortal film performance as Dr. Hill is peerless and unsurpassed. A total phony, a serial plagiarist with style, and the unctuous gallows charm of an undertaker, his true nature doesn't show itself until after he's decapitated and brought back to life. There's a paradoxical joie de vivre he displays during his zombie phase; unfettered by morality, he embodies his true nature as a monstrous creature of pure id and naked desire, fearless, free and strangely, never more alive.

Stuart's mastery of live theater accrued by his many years running the Organic Theatre Company helped us immensely while rehearsing. Every rehearsal began with a theater game, usually some form of improv. This is rare in professional theater. His desire to continually refine and improve the show was consuming. During many weeks of preview performances, he took notes directly from the audience every night. Over its four years on stage in Los Angeles, New York, Edinburgh and Las Vegas I was decapitated 200 times. And 200 performances in, Stu was still giving notes before every performance. When we took the show to Edinburgh and did 25 performances in 30 days, Stu ran the lighting board for every show. The ultimate team player.

There's a strange meta-theatricality that arises from developing an iconic film for the stage. So many moments are deeply embedded in the psyche of horror fans. The zombie cat attack, the first corpse reanimation gone awry, the decapitation of Dr. Hill and his wicked deeds as a reanimated creature...all these are well established in our horror gestalt, bubbling up from primal fears and hungers.

There was unmitigated joy when presenting beloved, terrifying moments from a cherished film to fans who would see and recognize them, lovingly set to song and live action. Dr. Hill provided an enviable canvas to work with. In a sense, he became a much larger character on stage than in the film simply because he had so many songs. In a song or aria, the drama often stops completely so we can suspend the moment to look inside characters and see their emotional lives. The musical Dr. Hill was gifted with far more text than Hill in the film; we get to hear him sing a twisted, hypnotic serenade to Meg after her father is lobotomized ("If You're Ever Lonely"), he confronts West to steal his serum and delights in his fearless plagiarism, taunting him in an irresistible tango duet before getting bloodily decapitated and brought back to life ("I Will Be Famous"), and so on. Mark Nutter, our brilliant composer and lyricist, wrote so many terrific songs that there's very little dialogue. He'd worked with Stuart and the Organic Theatre in the 1970s and brought the perfect tone; pithy wordplay as clever as Gilbert or Sondheim combined with infectious tunes worthy of Broadway.

Working with original talents from the film was a special pleasure. Legendary FX artists John Beuchler, Tony Doublin and John Naulin all contributed essential parts to our bloody enterprise: zombie masks, cat puppets, scenery built for illusions and body switching, exploding eyeballs and hoses to pump blood on the crowd and, of course, the iconic syringes with glowing green serum.

The film was the best resource of all; everything we needed was already there. David Gale brought nuanced, truthful acting, perverse charm and that divinely mellifluous voice to his Dr. Hill. When he reaches his reanimated transformation and apotheosis, it's such a departure from the stuffy academic we first met that it still shocks every time. I don't look much like Gale and my approach to the character was not exactly imitative or mimetic, but rather informed by admiration for his performance and a desire to evoke his spirit, offering tribute to his unique character. I felt particularly inspired by his mesmeric, flashing eyes and snarling, predatory teeth, incorporating those elements into my own version.

What sticks with me most about the film isn't the eye popping gore and grue, the rapid pace and inexorable momentum of the unfolding story, nor even the unforgettable visual pun during the climax, it's the compelling, fully committed characters and how strongly they feel about each other. Their relationships, grounded in truth, provide a tentpole of reality around which all the insanity, violence and otherworldly zombie chaos can revolve and hold their orbits without ever spinning free into farce or pantomime. Somehow, a tale of reanimated corpses running riot becomes a true event, holding us in its thrall until the final, shocking moment.

Jeffrey Combs' star turn as Herbert West is rightly celebrated and iconic. Stu said that Jeff as an actor wears his soul on the outside, and I think that's exactly right. There's something utterly engrossing about watching him inhabit any role, especially one as dynamic and unstoppable as West. Barbara Crampton is perfectly cast as Meg, and lies at the very heart of the film. Her performance is one of the most nuanced, finely crafted and, ultimately, devastating of the decade and the genre. Bruce Abbott as Dan Cain is the unsung hero of the film; he's an instantly sympathetic actor full of natural charisma. If the audience doesn't accept the deep love of Dan and Meg, the story collapses. Dan opens and closes the film and the tale. He carries the narrative - the audience is on his journey, not West's - and the competing interests of his passionate love for Meg and his consuming desire to help patients by conquering death is the central conflict, the very crux of the drama.

The Original Cast Album for the musical was completed in 2016, and I'm impatient to see its release. With any luck, the show will be reanimated some day, perhaps in a new, unexpected form...

THE BIRDS

BY

WENDY MEDRANO

Festival Founder/Writer/Graphic Artist/
Artistic Director/Producer
Zed Fest Film Festival
Facebook: @ZedFest Twitter: @ZedFestFilmFest
ZedFest.org

Not many know my personal story about growing up in two different countries. Starting at the age of two, I began splitting my time between California and Central America, where I lived with my grandparents. They were two of the best people in the world; they loved food, music, and movies.

They taught me to appreciate classic films from a very early age, making Sunday evenings our regular cinema night. We would go to the local movie revival theater every Sunday night and catch old movies being screened for the first time in years on the big screen.

Some months, they would do all action, comedy, or horror movies. My grandfather was a big fan of the action, but it was my grandmother that taught me the brilliance of Hitchcock. We saw them all. She was great at figuring out the plot right at the start of the movie. She later told me, "Hitchcock knew how to spin a good yarn." I have to agree with her. After the screening, we would go to the local ice cream parlor Salon Rosa. While eating a banana split between all three of us, we would spend hours talking about the movies we saw.

I especially love *The Birds* because it has a woman at the center of the story. She wasn't playing a supportive, or a subordinate role. Melanie Daniels is the main person in this film. This is great from the beginning to the very climactic end, where she must lead a group of children to safety away from the birds.

Some viewers are divided on the story of *The Birds*. Were the people of this little isolated town fine until our main character showed up? On the other hand, some viewers say she exposes something odd and dormant in this creepy little island town. No matter what theory you have, we all agree that the birds themselves are terrifying and intriguing at the same time.

This film is audibly and visually frightening. I have this thing about sounds, so this movie really scares and creeps me out at the same time. There is no music, only Bernard Herrmann's orchestration of electronically enhanced bird sounds on an instrument called a Trautonium, creating a cacophony adding to the disquieting effect.

The suspense and horror are very well balanced in *The Birds*. The characters all have their own personal issues they're grappling with while they're trying to escape the physical threat of the birds. I've seen this film many times, and any time it's on, I have to watch it. Each time I watch it, I always see something new or catch something new to think about.

After watching it as an adult recently, I could relate to the Melanie Daniels character. She was the outsider in that town, being looked at with some suspicion because she was different. I know what that feels like, because as I said, I grew up between two places. I was considered an outsider in both. While I was in school here, I was a strange kid because I was Latin, bookish, and I really liked old movies.

I was also a sporty tomboy that was in both soccer and baseball teams. Most of my friends were boys and we really liked scary movies. My friends and I shared many good times watching scary movies and talking about them. While I lived in Central America I was also an outsider because I spoke English and was from California. Plus my grandparents were my guardians, so that made me different too.

Through it all, my affinity for books, music, and movies helped me feel like I wasn't so different or weird. Even if I was weird, that was not necessarily a bad thing. In many ways, I feel it's an asset because I see things others don't and it helps me be more creative. The love of movies is what led me to begin this great journey I'm on: running Zedfest, an independent film festival with great storytelling done on a low budget.

I also think It's important for me to focus on women filmmakers and strong lead female protagonists in the films we screen. Seeing *The Birds* as a kid was one of the first times I saw a movie with a woman not being the secondary character. In fact, this movie has four female stories at the forefront. We have the Melanie Daniels character, Lydia Brenner (the mother), Annie Hayworth (ex-fiancée and school teacher) and Cathy Brenner (the little sister). It's very unusual for a movie of that era (and a movie now) to have so many female characters being explored. We see Mitch Brenner's character deal with his overbearing mother, played by Jessica Tandy. Through the course of the film, we find out why he never married the nice schoolteacher. His mother had objected to all his romantic choices. Mrs. Brenner is domineering and needy at the same time. She emotionally manipulates him into not being able to live full-time in his San Francisco apartment. He is forced to go home every weekend to Bodega Bay to take care of his mother and sister. Because his father died almost five years ago, he feels he has to be the caretaker of the family. His younger sister Cathy, who is a preteen, is beginning to notice the odd relationship he has with their mother. Cathy is open to Melanie Daniels as a new friend for herself, and for Mitch. When they meet, Melanie and Mitch start a witty and playful teasing type of exchange. They soon become intrigued and attracted to one another. This seems to scare his mother, because she wants to keep him with her (and to not have anything else change after her husband's death).

Throughout the course of the film, we start to learn more about Melanie Daniels--why she is so aloof and guarded. She was raised by a newspaper publishing single father, who is presumably a pretty busy person, so she had to learn to fend for herself. As a result, she winds up hanging out with a bunch of superficial people, until a public embarrassing incident causes her to question her life choices. She begins to see that she should find more meaning in her life as a constructive member of society. She has had to learn that people are going to think what they want about you, so if you're true to yourself and you know who you are, let them think what they want and your true friends and family will know the type of person you are. She is beginning this new stage in her life when she stumbles upon this freak occurrence and the little town of Bodega Bay.

The townspeople add a lot to the story because they seem very closed off to new people. In many movies and books where the woman is the main protagonist, there is always some suspicion voiced by one or more of the characters in the story. In this film, another woman in a diner scene says, "I think you're evil, this is all happening because of you." Melanie slaps her to make her stop, but I think like many of us in this situation, being blamed unfairly for a freak occurrence would make you force the woman to stop accusing you. This is a very powerful moment, and it kind of shows a glimpse of the main character's inner fighting spirit.

I recently heard a funny theory of the duality of the title of this movie. Alfred Hitchcock was British born, and bird is British slang for a girl or young woman. This theory is doubtful, but funny to think about.

The Birds was based on a short story by the same name, written by Daphne du Maurier and published in 1952, also focusing on a series of real-life, sudden, unexplained, violent bird attacks on the people of Bodega Bay, California over the course of a few days. Ms. Du Maurier became interested in this event and began crafting personal stories around it. Perhaps, there are many female lead characters because it was based on a story written by a woman. Her stories often featured very strong and fascinating women, like the characters in *Rebecca* and *My Cousin Rachel*, Daphne du Maurier's other novels. Hitchcock was a big fan of hers, directing another film, *Jamaica Inn*, based on the novel by the same name. I think *The Birds*, based on her short story, is the best adaptation of her work by Alfred Hitchcock. I wish he had directed a version of *My Cousin Rachel*. It would have been amazing.

The great thing about good films is that you can see them at different times in your life and be able to relate to different characters, depending on what stage in life you're going through.

This film is also well written, produced and acted. Years after my first time viewing *The Birds*, I can still vividly remember how it felt. When I see it now, it is still a powerful film. The best thing is that it reminds me of the great times I shared with my grandparents. They played such an important part in my life and they taught me to appreciate good movies.

At the time, it was not a done deal that *The Birds* would be a success or that new film fans would discover it many years after its initial release. Hitchcock's film team were attempting new tricks and traveling down new territory. The budget was getting out of control, and people were beginning to doubt Hitchcock's genius as a filmmaker. He believed in his team and the work they were doing. It's difficult to be the first and to innovate. But if you're like Hitchcock and his team, you know what you're working on every day. It's looking great and it feels right. In the end, he was a film fan. He would excitedly observe how things were coming together, driving the team to fight to complete the project, no matter the extra time and costs. He was usually a stickler for storyboards and not improvising scenes, but during this film shoot, he improvised some scenes because he wanted the movie to be as powerful and visceral as possible.

It's amazing how this movie is still influencing horror filmmakers many years later. I have to give a nod to Alfred Hitchcock's film team. He was one of the first filmmakers to set up a team like that, who focused on visuals, audio, practical effects, and style. They were very dedicated to innovating how we saw horror on the big screen. Their influence is clear to this day. This is why I chose *The Birds* as my favorite horror film, because it should be appreciated for the groundbreaking work they did.

Hitchcock really could spin a good yarn…

THE CURSE OF THE FACELESS MAN

BY

DEL HOWISON

Writer/Editor/Shop Owner/Purveyor of Nightmares

Dark Delicacies, Midian Unmade

The Survival of Margaret Thomas

Twitter: @DarkDel Facebook: @DarkDelicacies

DarkDel.com

A nature-created mummy that pushes its own way out of the grave of an ancient city excavation was a cheap black-and-white combination of the *Dracula* love-from-beyond-the-grave idea, mashed with yet another redo of *The Mummy* taking place in Italy instead of Egypt. It was also my first experience as a young child seeing a horror film in a Saturday matinee, sans the emotional protection of my parents. I was surrounded by my peers and had to put up a bold front of bravery while peeking through my fingers held up in front of my face. I was scared shitless, and since those were the days when I ate my popcorn swimming in butter, my face was covered in greasy streaks from my protective fingers. I saw everything behind my fleshy defensive screen. When I walked out with the other kids that afternoon, my life had changed. *The Curse of the Faceless Man* left its pumice-streaked hole of emotion, fear and desire in my life, and I have spent the entirety of my years trying to fill that hole and escape the clutches of horror to live a normal life. I'm a lucky man to not have managed that.

Elaine Edwards (who also appeared in *The Bat* with Vincent Price and *The Purple Gang* with Barry Sullivan) was so beautiful that, being the impressionable boy that I was (I saw it in matinee in 1964), I could understand why Quintillus Aurelius, an Etruscan gladiator slave who was tortured and sentenced to death for daring to fall in love with a woman he should not have fallen in love with, would come back from the grave to reclaim her...or at least a woman who looked like her and happened to be interested in Pompeii. She was the fiancée of one of the doctors involved in the archeology project near the museum. A doctor of what, I'm not sure I ever knew (archeology I suppose). Poor Quint loved her then, but when the mountain blew its top, he could not escape his jail cell, and thus became one of the many mummified bodies left behind by Vesuvius's eruption.

So, Volcano Man and many other articles are dug up in Pompeii and trucked to a museum which is equipped with a research lab for such things. They were always digging up some old shit in those days. The doctors, including actor Richard Anderson (who showed up later in my youth on TV's *The Six Million Dollar Man* and *The Bionic Woman*) run X-rays and all sorts of scientifically-looking chemical tests on this perfectly preserved man (well, except for the fact that he has no face, but that just seemed to be a minor inconvenience). In the meantime, people keep getting knocked off, and every time a slow-reaching ash-covered hand inched around a corner to grab somebody by the throat, my own hand flew up in front of my face, fingers spread - of course - so that I didn't miss a moment behind my protection.

Like any good mummy film, this one is filled with curses – one of which has our visiting heroine living in the very house that Mummy Man cursed before his death – the "house on the fourth hill." And better yet, there's a cursed medallion which bears the overly long description, "The house on the fourth hill of Pompeii shall fall. Its people shall perish, and whatsoever stands between me and what is mine shall perish. I visit the curse upon thee until eternity…the fires of the Earth shall consume them. I am the son of Etruscan. I will live when the Roman is no more. Quintillus Aurelius." As any kid at a matinee knows, there is no escaping a curse as diabolical as that one. I did begin to get the idea that sex and horror were compatible bedmates. I just didn't know how to put it together yet. This, of course, was explained a few years later as I watched Hammer fare when I was older.

However, I was hooked on horror after that, going to matinees to catch every horror film I could, or sneaking downstairs to watch late-night scary films after my parents had gone to bed. I gave up that last bit after sitting alone in the dark and watching a color film which took place in a dusty old castle (was it *Nightmare Castle*?) where they strapped a two-sided cage on some guy's face that held a rat on the other side. When the cage's divider was pulled up, the hungry rat ran over and started eating the guy's face while he screamed the entire time. That was it. I ran upstairs and back to bed, leaving the late night films alone until I'd gotten a little older.

The Saturday matinees at the local theaters I grew up near, The Redford (where they later premiered *The Evil Dead*) and The Royal in Detroit, opened an entirely new world to me. The smell of popcorn and the screaming audiences filled with kids will stay with me forever. Each film I saw was like reading a new book – another world emerged – and in my mind it was being presented only for me.

A wonderful thing was that the very next time I went to the matinee after seeing *The Curse of the Faceless Man*, I was treated to Tony Randall's scenery-chewing performance in *The*

Seven Faces of Dr. Lao, where he played all the characters including Dr. Lao, The Abominable Snowman, Merlin the Magician, Apollonius of Tyana, Pan, The Giant Serpent, and Medusa, in full color. With a script by Charles Beaumont, based on a novel by Charles G. Finney, this film allowed me to see how the combination of fantasy and horror worked together. I knew I was seeing something very special and life-changing even at that young age. It opened another door in my hallway of awareness.

AN AMERICAN WEREWOLF IN LONDON

BY

JOSH STAPLES

Musician, Illustrator, Designer, Podcast Host
Forever Midnight Podcast, The New Trust, The Velvet Teen
TheNewTrust.com ForeverMidnight.net
Instagram: @JJStapes

For any movie lover, choosing a single favorite film can be heartbreaking. You gotta quickly pare down the list of every movie you've seen, (apologizing to the movies that don't make the cut, because, of course, the movie's feelings are hurt), and then perform millisecond-long mental scans of each film in the remaining handful for further triage. When picking a favorite horror film in particular, the criteria we use for choosing gets even narrower and we start inserting caveats: stuff like "that movie is more science fiction than horror," or "that one's too popular and people will think I'm lame if I say it's my favorite," and (again considering the movie's feelings for some weird reason) "enough people love that one already." This whole sequence occurs while choosing our favorite films in casual, private conversation. So, when you know that shit's gonna be in print, the pressure is on. You gotta choose the one film that makes you look cool, smart, and of unique character: the obscure deep cut that's under-appreciated, hyper-stylish, critically contentious and practically too-rare-to-view...or, you can stop acting like such a dilly, and start from scratch.

Which movie is the one that you simply love watching, never get tired of watching, and look forward to watching again because it stirs your emotions and thrills your senses? Personally, that movie is John Landis' 1981 masterpiece, *An American Werewolf In London.*

When I first saw *An American Werewolf in London* (let's just call it *Werewolf* from here on out), it was a rented VHS copy played on an ailing tube-television through a fifty-pound, top-loading VCR, which my family had on permanent loan from some generous, wealthy friends. I was probably 10 years old and the year was 1984, so the luxury of watching movies at home - unedited and uninterrupted by commercials - was practically brand new. We were also close friends with another family who owned a VCR, whose two kids were younger than I was. Nevertheless, my sister and I would watch our first scary movies with them at their house. We started with milder titles like *Creepshow* and *Something Wicked This Way Comes*, but quickly we were onto heavier stuff - mostly by way of a solitary (legendary) bootleg videocassette duped in LP mode, containing *Alien*, *The Thing*, and *Poltergeist*. Granted, we often speed-watched the first two darker films while fast-forwarding to *Poltergeist*, which, at the time, was hands-down my favorite movie, alongside *E.T.*, which came out the same month (call me nuts, but something about those two movies had a similar vibe).

My parents split up in the early 1980s, and after a couple of years (and a couple bogus boyfriends), my mom started dating a very cool guy (a friend of the aforementioned legendary-VHS tape-owning-family) named Gary. Gary was a New Yorker living in San Francisco, where he worked for an architectural firm and moonlighted as an amateur stand-up comic. He stood six-three and drove a tiny convertible Fiat that he could barely fit inside, even less so with two fifty-pound, blonde whelps in the practically non-existent backseat. During the time that Gary was courting my mom, he would witness us kids watching these same few horror movies over and over, countless times. One night on a video-store outing, he rented *An American Werewolf* for us to watch at home. Gary had seen it in the theater a couple years before and thought the whole family might like it. I had never heard of it, but I was stoked to see any new horror movie, even if it was a werewolf movie. I'd seen pictures of werewolves in my dad's tattered, yellowed volumes of *Famous Monsters* magazines, but didn't know anything about the werewolf legend, and the stills of dudes with hair glued to their faces never really scared me.

With the opening scene of *Werewolf*, we are introduced to David and Jack, American students hopping out of a shepherd's truck while hitchhiking across the English countryside. Their dialogue is realistic, natural and funny, and the scene takes its time, letting us get to know these characters and their relationship as they trek across the moors at dusk. Immediately, I'm enthralled by the lives of Jack and David (played by Griffin Dunne and David Naughton, respectively). It's like eavesdropping on the cool and funny older kids at the video arcade, but they're out of their element, plopped into this desolate green hillside. Like *Poltergeist*, it's a long, casual look at these true to life characters of their time, and in their skin...just before all hell breaks loose.

We all must know how this movie goes by now: Jack and David arrive at The Slaughtered Lamb, get turned back out into the darkness, and are viciously attacked by a werewolf. Right up until the grizzly assault, they're joking with each other - even while terrified - just like any of us would. Jack is attacked, and David flees in fear - shameful, but very likely what any of us would do, right? This is what makes *Werewolf* as harrowing for me to watch now as it was at 10 - the sympathy I have for these young people and what's happening to them. Along with some of the greatest special effects of all time, courtesy of Rick Baker, it's what makes David's iconic werewolf transformation seem all the more painful - that we know him and we like him.

There is so much to love about this movie: the fun and colorful characters, the unexpected and shocking violence of the initial attack, some unrivaled surreal and chaotic dream sequences set to a haunting score, the sweet love story between David and Nurse Price (played wonderfully by Jenny Agutter), Jack's many returns from the grave, the unreal transformation and subsequent horror of David's wolf-out rampage and the Benny Hill-style comedy of the morning after, the lascivious Piccadilly porno theatre as David watches the hilarious "See You Next Wednesday" while receiving suicide tips from his gory, undead victims and Jack. Landis gets everything right with this groundbreaking horror film and delivers it all with a wry sense of humor, a banging soundtrack and truly realistic characters that we - at least I - can empathize with. Not only did Werewolf scare the shit out of me, I knew that it was super cool, funny and sweet. I hadn't then, and still haven't seen another film quite like it.

I've watched *Werewolf* many times over the years. I think I can see past the nostalgia that the movie holds for me and still love it every time. When I finally saw it on a big silver screen (I had only watched it on televisions for most of my life), I realized how much of the film I hadn't actually seen. In many shots, the werewolf will appear very small on the huge screen, and was practically invisible on a tiny TV. *American Werewolf* still holds up to me as one of the best films of the 1980s, period. But really, why should I separate the nostalgia from the legitimate reasons to love this film? Gary (who would become my stepdad a couple years later) had introduced this film to me not just because it's a horror film, but probably because of the humorous parts, and perhaps because he could also relate to young men far from home. Watching *Werewolf* with Gary endeared me to him early on. I can't separate those early memories from the film, and can't think of a reason why I should.

Getting to talk about movies with my forever-homeys, Jef and Brian on our show, *Forever Midnight* is an absolute blast. It's given me cause to enjoy many films I might not otherwise watch, and although I don't have trouble recognizing good things in all movies (when they're available), John Landis had raised a very high bar when he created *An American Werewolf In London* against which I compare most movies. As co-hosts of a horror-focused podcast, we've also been able to sit down with many of the people involved in making some of our all-time favorite movies. For example, our first guest on the show was Michael Grais, the screenwriter of *Poltergeist*, a film I've probably mentioned in this essay as many times as the film I actually chose. We once interviewed William Katt of Brian De Palma's *Carrie* (or even more nostalgic for me, *The Greatest American Hero*), and a couple of years ago, we found ourselves sitting across a table and talking into microphones with David Naughton, himself. Yes, he's just as funny and sweet as the David he portrays in the film. As he talked about his experiences working in England with John Landis on this film that I've been watching steadily and lovingly for thirty years, I remembered to pause for a few seconds to clearly think, "Wait until Gary hears about this."

THE SHINING (1980)

BY

YAN BIRCH

Actor/Producer

The People Under The Stairs, Charmed,
Slumber Party Massacre lll, Sky Sharks, Agramon's Gate

Instagram: @YanBirchPage Facebook/Twitter: @YanBirch

My favorite horror movie is *The Shining* by the genius filmmaker Stanley Kubrick. Being quite young the first time I saw it, I became spellbound by the eerie energy throughout (even way before it became visibly scary on screen). Mr. Kubrick was somehow able to provide me a feeling of discomfort from the first frame to the last. It was his signature in brilliantly making a great horror film. The first time I ever had that feeling was when I watched *The Birds* by Alfred Hitchcock, another awesome film by a great filmmaker. I really enjoyed *The Shining* as we followed the family down a darkly psychotic ride, led by an amazing performance by Jack Nicholson (whom I had the absolute gratifying and memorable pleasure of meeting once).

From the start of the film, I was immediately sucked into the characters and why they were in their situation: staying in a desolate, deserted mountain resort over a hard winter, chosen by Jack's character. Having gone sober after a violent episode with his son and family, this experience was an attempt to bring them together and rebuild their trust. When we learn that a former employee killed his family under suspicious and unexplained circumstances while taking care of the resort, it was immediately obvious that something very wrong was happening. The best part is how subtly this was portrayed by Kubrick. I was riveted to the screen from the start of the film.

Later on in life and years after I'd seen the film, I had the pleasure to work with such greats as Roger Corman on *Slumber Party Massacre III*, and as the Stairmaster in Wes Craven's *The People Under the Stairs* (which incidentally was my absolute breakthrough to a worldwide audience). That film brought me so many opportunities for more work and the opportunity to meet horror fans all around the world. I am so very grateful for this. When I worked with Chuck Russell on his film *Bless The Child*, I realized that there are certain directors and writers that can really translate a great horror story from paper to screen. I was not fortunate enough to ever work with Mr. Stanley Kubrick, but as I mentioned, I have been very fortunate to have had the opportunity to work with other legends in the horror community. Okay...back to *The Shining*. I must emphasize that it was groundbreaking in the sense that the audience wasn't sure if some of the characters were dead or alive. It was done in such a way, that when I saw it for the second time, I had to rewind the VHS (I know, it dates me a little, LOL). Everyone wondered about the mental state of some of the characters. In my opinion, it was done so well and for those days it was rarely unique. It was not until much later that I felt the same way when the new guy on the block, M. Night Shyamalan, made *The Sixth Sense*. "Do I see dead people," or not? Mr. Kubrick was hands down something else, so ahead of his time and very insightful to the complexities of the human psyche. He translated the written page into celluloid in such a smooth and effortless way that made the depth and emotion in each frame feel real. I know it's a movie, but WTF…I am right there…I feel it! Years later, when I was reading the *A Nightmare on Elm Street 3: Dream Warriors* script, I was strongly reminded of the way Kubrick expressed himself. It caught me in a way nothing had done for a while. It felt so real and authentic.

Another thing that Mr. Kubrick did so brilliantly was to involve children in describing the supernatural situations at hand. Almost right away, when we get to the resort, we learn through a child's eyes that there might be more to this place than we are told! This brings up another similarity to Wes Craven in the horror world. Nobody had ever cast a young black kid as the hero before Wes. It was revolutionary. I loved that fact alone.

One of my absolute favorite scenes in *The Shining* is when Danny rides his tricycle down the hallway…it's so very creepy, and oh, don't get me started on the dead young twin sisters, played by real twins Lisa and Louise Burns (whom I've had the pleasure of meeting at a horror convention some years back). Things just start to unravel from that point. It's such a rollercoaster, brain twister, and suspenseful adventure with just enough elements to make it work, that I feel this was, and is, a true masterpiece of filmmaking. My hats off to Mr. Stanley Kubrick. In the future, I hope to work with more creative forces as dedicated to the art as he was, creating projects similar to this great one, which is one of my all-time favorite movies, and, for sure, my favorite horror movie!!!

PHOTO BY: W.B. FONTENOT

NEAR DARK

BY

MATTHEW CURRIE HOLMES

Writer/Director/Producer/Actor

The Curse of Buckout Road, Traces, Wrong Turn 2, The Fog

Twitter/Instagram: @Mch2k

I have been obsessed with movies and storytelling since childhood.

I may not remember what I ate yesterday and often can't remember birthdays or your kid's name, but when it comes to seeing a film, my hippocampus sucks in everything about the experience.

I saw *Star Wars* in the theater with my three uncles in 1978. I was four years old, but I can tell you what each of them was wearing. In 1982, my dad and I scrounged up all the spare change in the house so we could see a double bill of *They Call Me Bruce* and *Enter the Dragon*. We loaded up on snacks, took the train and saw both films on a rainy Saturday afternoon matinee. A decade later, I walked out of *Reservoir Dogs* with half the dialogue already memorized (and terrorized everyone I knew with it for months).

Yup, when it comes to movies, actors, directors, cinematographers, screenwriters...this is what occupies most of my mental real estate. What follows is a story of the one that got away and the vindication that followed.

At 13 my family moved to London, Ontario, Canada. What a fucking bite that was. Newly a teen, coming into my own, and not an acquaintance in sight. It was summertime and it was impossible to break into the tight cliques at our rent-controlled townhouse complex. I retreated to the local mom & pop video store called Cinema City. I watched anything and everything they had that summer, so I entered eighth grade with a near-encyclopedic knowledge of late '70s and early '80s movies.

In October that same year, I saw a TV ad for a movie that was "coming this Friday to a theater near you." The TV spot was short, about thirty seconds or so. It featured a striking image of a filthy young boy wearing a trench coat, illuminated by a match en route to a cigarette. Then a wide shot of a mist-covered hill suddenly topped by the silhouettes of six ominous figures. Some quick cuts: gunshots, the roasting flesh of some dude running, the beating sun blazing down from the Oklahoma sky. Then the late, great Bill Paxton, covered in blood, climbing onto the grill of a moving 18-wheel rig. He slams his fist into the hood and yanks out wires and tubes! All of this before the title fades in and that trailer guy's gravelly voice says:

"*Near Dark*...pray for daylight."

Holy fucking shit! Who was that kid? Why was that guy running like he was on fire? Are these VAMPIRES? Was that kid smoking?? I have to see this movie RIGHT NOW. I had officially found my new obsession.

When *Near Dark* opened in my town, it played for ONE WEEK at a 2-screen bijou cinema called The Capitol. It was paired with *Hellraiser* and *Fatal Attraction* was on the other screen, taking up both the 7 & 9 o'clock time slots.

I remember gliding past the poster as I rode my skateboard down Dundas Street...Bill Paxton wearing a badass leather jacket...his face bloody and burnt, these small shafts of light piercing through his flesh. I mean, COME ON. I had to see this movie!!

But it was not meant to be. Unlike the United States, Canada has a very restrictive film ratings system. If a movie is rated 'R' you CANNOT see it unless you are over 18. In the case of *Near Dark*, I couldn't even pay for something less restrictive and then sneak in (something I did countless times as a youth), because that R-rated juggernaut of a blockbuster *Fatal Attraction* was taking up the theater's second screen! It was clear that The Capitol was a no-go for the kiddies this particular week in October. A week later the marquee read *Princess Bride* and (still) *Fatal Attraction*. I was crushed! *Near Dark* was gone forever, as was my hope of ever seeing it on the big screen. I'd have to wait for the damned thing to come out on video.

After The Cure, skateboarding, and girls, my passion was movies. My memories of the late '80s cannot be separated from *The Lost Boys*, *A Nightmare on Elm Street 3*, and *Evil Dead II: Dead By Dawn*. In the spring of 1988, I contracted an extremely rare disease called Henoch-Schönlein Purpura. HSP is a disease that effects the kidneys and skin, and it caused me so much pain I couldn't walk unassisted. I could no longer manage stairs or my skateboard...so the family living room became my bedroom. My only source of activity was the excruciatingly painful walk across the street to Cinema City to rent movies. This would be my entire summer: alone, all day, watching rented video cassettes. Déjà vu. In retrospect it was, I suppose, ideal training for a burgeoning film nerd...but for a 14-year-old boy about to enter high school, the double whammy of my disease and obsession with horror films was social suicide.

Around that same time, I started collecting *GoreZone Magazine*, the bi-monthly companion to *Fangoria*. *GoreZone* (for those too young to remember) was the more "extreme" horror magazine with an emphasis on special effects makeup.

Each gloriously gory issue featured a 2-sided centerfold poster from a movie featuring particularly gruesome or intricate special effects. Whenever a new *GoreZone* came out, I immediately removed the poster and carefully taped it to my bedroom wall. I often bought TWO copies so I could display the images on both sides of the centerfold: *Pumpkinhead*, Freddy Krueger, *Phantasm*, Pinhead & Female Cenobite, *RoboCop*, and deeper cuts like Renny Harlin's *Prison* were plastered floor-to-ceiling in my bedroom (and now, around the couch). And with every issue, a new trip to the video store was in order. Lesser-known titles like *The Unnamable*, *Lair of the White Worm*, *Basket Case*, *Re-Animator* and *Prison* came into my world, and were then sourced and voraciously consumed, thanks to *GoreZone Magazine*.

After almost two months on the living room sofa-bed, a *GoreZone* arrived featuring a centerfold poster of BILL PAXTON HIMSELF, burned to a crisp, wearing a leather jacket. Hey, it was a poster for that movie I was obsessed with last October! Then, it really sunk in: holy shit...this was *Near Dark*. It had been long enough since the theatrical release for this thing to have come out on VHS.

I grabbed my crutches and limped my HSP ass to Cinema City. (It took me fifteen minutes to exit the house, cross the road, and finally collapse against the video store counter.) Owned by a chain smoking Dutch man named Tony, Cinema City was the kind of place where you could sit and talk about film for hours. The XXX movies lived on the top shelf, and the NEW RELEASE wall not only featured the big Hollywood hits, but fantastic foreign fare and amazing, obscure art films. Because Tony was a true cineaste, he always carried the unrated versions of films whenever possible, twisted, *GoreZone*-approved movies included.

I asked Tony if he had *Near Dark*. "Ah the Kaserine Beegalow movie. Yes, it's on the wall, ovah zerr." He pointed to a side section titled Horror. Even on crutches I beat him to the VHS box, and he retrieved the videocassette from the shelves behind the register. "Zis is really good. You're gonna like it." He put a fitted plastic clip reading "RENTED" on the empty box, put it back in the Horror section, and lit a cigarette (it was the '80s). I left him blowing smoke out his nose like a dragon as I hobbled out of the store as fast as I could. Our obligatory hour-long chat about movies would have to wait until next time.

Near Dark tells the story about Caleb Colton (Adrian Pasdar), a restless young man from Oklahoma who meets the mysterious and utterly captivating Mae (Jenny Wright) one night in front of a small-town liquor store. Caleb falls for Mae swearing he "ain't never seen a girl like [her]".

The two of them spend the night driving around in Caleb's old truck, falling in love. They lose track of time and Mae starts to panic because the sun is coming up. She bites Caleb on the neck, hops out of the truck and runs through a vast, dusty field. Caleb begins to get really sick and he stumbles home on foot. The rising sun causes Caleb's flesh to smoke and burn, and, just when you think he's done for, an RV pulls up beside Caleb and yanks him inside.

Inside the RV we meet a "family" of nomadic American vampires lead by the charismatic Jesse Hooker (played to perfection by eternal badass Lance Henriksen). "Uncle" Severen (the scene stealing Bill Paxton) threatens to kill Caleb...until Mae tells them all that "He's been bit, but he ain't been bled." Jesse, along with his soft-featured yet sadistic "wife" Diamondback (stone-cold killer, Jeanette Goldstein) and their young "son" Homer (Joshua John Miller) agree to give Caleb a week to make his first kill. If he does, he will earn a place in the family.

What follows is a blistering, fast-paced neo-western horror movie that is part family drama and part dustbowl action film, with the freshest take on the vampire genre I have ever seen.

The coven steal cars and travel from dusty small town to dusty small town killing hitchhikers, truck drivers, an unsuspecting passerby...there seems to be no real method to their murderous ways other than that they are creatures of the night who feed to live and live to feed.

Along the way, we discover snippets of their past, we watch Mae and Caleb fall deeper in love, and wait with mounting tension to see if Caleb has what it takes to kill and become one of them. This all builds to a beautiful and violent climax: a ten-minute sequence (almost 15% of the film's total running time) involving a small country bar in the middle of nowhere, where the patrons are served up like fattened pigs to the slaughter. The scene ends with a terrified teenage cowboy (James LeGross) being presented to Caleb like a sacrificial lamb.

What I found most striking about this scene is that, until this point in the film, the vampires had hunted alone...but the scene's opening shot, a mist-shrouded hill crested by six ominous silhouettes, tells us that these nomads also hunt as a pack. The scene is vicious and brutal, but filled with wit and gallows humor: you can't help but cheer this undead family on. All the violence that follows is perfectly choreographed to a fantastic cover of "Fever" by The Cramps.

Lacking the sociopathic tendencies required to kill indiscriminately, Caleb's righteousness is both the moral center of, and the main conflict in *Near Dark*. Everything comes to a head when Caleb refuses to kill LeGross, which comes back to bite the family in the ass during the film's most exhilarating scene involving a daytime shootout at an old roadside motel.... But I'll stop there. I don't want to spoil it if you have yet to see this masterpiece.

For my money, the *Near Dark* screenplay by Kathryn Bigelow & Eric Red is essentially perfect. It's concise, unapologetic and sets up a mythology that subverts the vampire genre...It takes what we're used to seeing: the romantic, glossy fantasy, hypnotic hyperbole, and turns it on its ear. These vampires aren't flawless or sexy...they're grimy nomads who steal cars and check into fleabag motels off the roadside. Absent are the eloquent and entitled musings of Lestat or the pinings of a lovelorn Dracula. These folks are poor white trash rednecks, and they like it! (Fun Fact: the word "vampire" is never once mentioned in the movie.)

The direction, from then-first-time filmmaker (now Oscar winner) Kathryn Bigelow is sure-footed, bold, and doesn't meander in the slightest. This is one auspicious directorial debut, and I'd be remiss if I didn't mention, in the same section, the flawless cinematography by Adam Greenberg. His visual storytelling is superb, from the beautifully constructed shot where Caleb is drinking from Mae's wrist under the backdrop of two pump jacks, to that classic mist-shrouded hilltop scene...if you look closely you can see Jesse and Diamondback are clasping hands, descending the hill toward the murderous rage as a couple. These moments give us beautiful subtext without saying a single word.

Alone in the living room, I watched *Near Dark* three times that day and then again that night after my family had gone to bed. The screenplay, the cinematography, the most brutal violence...it all sucked me into an enthralling, suspenseful, and wholly thrilling vortex. On that day, that one movie made me forget that I had a disease. It made me forget that I was in constant pain. When *Near Dark* ended for the fourth time, I took a huge breath and knew I'd been through something that was changing the course of my life.

By the time September hit, I had rented *Near Dark* another half dozen times. Some of my skater buddies would swing by and I'd make them watch it, and they all became big fans. By October, I had rented *Near Dark* so many times that Tony gave it to me. I had that VHS tape for another two years, until some punk stole it during a B&E at our townhouse complex in 1990. My family lost a bunch of stuff in that robbery, but the loss of my *Near Dark* VHS was the biggest kick in the teeth (for me).

Is it any surprise that by my mid-20s, I was the manager of a small independent video store? During my tenure, I probably turned on at least 100 people to *Near Dark*. It was my secret weapon when trying to impress customers. This was, to steal a phrase from Elric Kane (one of the brilliant hosts of *Pure Cinema Podcast*), my "handshake movie." This film defined my taste, and if anyone else loved it as much as I did, I knew we could be friends.

To this day, I've probably seen *Near Dark* 85-90 times, and always on either VHS or DVD. I've contested many times over the years that this film is the white whale of theatrical viewings.

But on May 3rd 2019, it finally happened for me.

Unlike Ahab's golden doubloon taped to the mast, I caught my white whale when Los Angeles' New Beverly Cinema screened a gorgeous, nearly flawless 35mm print of *Near Dark*. It was glorious and having finally this Pièce De Résistance in the theater, I can say two things with absolute certainty:

1. *Near Dark* is a fucking timeless classic.
2. If the big screen treatment did anything to alter my perception of *Near Dark*, it absolutely solidified its ranking as my all-time favorite horror movie.

Have you seen it? You should.

EVIL DEAD II

BY

JENNIFER FOSTER

Synth Player

Pide Ayuda

PideAyuda.Bandcamp.com

Instagram: @JeneralSkant

One evening during the late 1980s to 1990, my family and I had some kind of function to attend. This function was held the same evening as one of the yearly *Comic Relief* specials on HBO (hosted by Whoopi Goldberg, fellow Long Beach, New York native Billy Crystal, and the gone-too-soon Robin Williams). In preparation, my parents programmed our VCR to record it. Since my parents also wanted to watch whatever movie immediately followed *Comic Relief*, they programed the VCR to record at a specific time and let it run until the tape eventually came to an end.

For the life of me, I can't remember the movie that followed *Comic Relief*. All I know is that the video cassette contained *Comic Relief*, some forgettable movie, and *Evil Dead II*. We didn't have an abundance of videos at home, and I was starting to realize that children's films weren't holding my interest like they used to. After watching whatever movie followed *Comic Relief*, which certainly contained R-rated content (because even at that time, "It's not TV, It's HBO"), *Evil Dead II* started. We get a brief history on the Book of the Dead. How fascinating to my young eyes! The opening title card reminded me of the video covers in the horror movie section at the local video store that used to captivate me. Sadly, I never went home with any of them as they were deemed too much for my sister and I at such a young age. I was so surprised to find this hidden treasure buried after the hours of programming my parents recorded. Jackpot!

At around 10 years old, I was completely enchanted. I laughed at Linda juggling her own head, the books, deer head and lamp coming to life, and Ash's possessed hand breaking plates on his head. I was terrified at the unknown presence that chased him through the halls, the unseen evil in the darkness of the woods - perhaps scarier because it couldn't be seen - and Henrietta in the cellar. Henrietta scared the hell out of me. Never at the time had anything frightened me more than the thought of being locked in a dark cellar with Henrietta. Hell, even Henrietta singing "Hush Little Baby," looking normal while peeking out through the cellar scared the hell out of me. Never before did a horror movie make me feel so many different emotions. The laughs were endless, the suspense nonstop, and I was scared.

An hour into watching, on the edge of my seat, I watched as Annie walked through the cabin with the dagger in her hand. After accidentally stabbing Jake (gasp! I thought he was already dead!), Evil Ash pops up in the window! Then, just as Annie drags Jake into the door and I hope she can close it in time... the tape stopped and started automatically rewinding. Imagine my disappointment in finding out there just wasn't enough room on the tape to record *Comic Relief*, the forgettable movie, and *Evil Dead II* in its entirety. Though many would consider the time spent watching a movie without seeing the last 20 something minutes a waste, once the tape finished rewinding, I fast-forwarded the tape through several hours of comedy and who-knows-what just to watch the first hour of this hilarious, suspenseful, scary movie all over again. I did this for years.

Since, as previously stated, my parents weren't particularly thrilled about renting horror movies for my sister and me, we weren't permitted to rent it. None of my friends had seen it. This was many years before easily searching for a movie through a search engine, streaming it online, or renting it myself. It was useless. I didn't know the end of *Evil Dead II* and was doomed to remain in limbo. I get to watch the greatest hour of horror I had seen without ever getting to know the end. ARE THEY ALL DEAD BY DAWN?

Now, as an adult, I look back on this with more love than I did even as a child watching it for the first time. I can fully appreciate how hilarious Bruce Campbell is. His performance is overacting at its finest: the melodrama, facial expressions, etc. would give Tommy Wiseau a run for his money. But Bruce is in on the joke: when he becomes emotional hearing the music his wife danced to before she died; his look of defeat when he sees the bridge is gone…all top notch. I always crack up when I hear him shout "GIVE ME BACK MY HAAAAAANNNNND!!!" The sound effects and makeup - excellent. And the fantastic music is used perfectly throughout the entire movie.

Years later, well into my teens, I went to a friend's house. Looking through their movie collection I noticed a copy of *Evil Dead II* on their shelf. "I love this movie!" I exclaimed. "Can we watch it?" Luckily my friend obliged.

Finally, at 16 years old, after watching the first hour over a hundred times, I was finally seeing the elusive last 20 minutes of my favorite horror movie, the one I had spent years obsessing over, ending be damned! This movie I still cherish to this day.

My friend inserted the tape into the VCR. Off we went!

I was just as crazy about the movie as the first time I saw

it. But this time, there was more! Annie was able to get the door closed! Whew! Ash is good again! Yes! Now he's battling Henrietta (and what the hell is up with her neck, oh my God)! Annie saying the words! Getting sucked into the portal! And then….

"Welp, I guess I have to see *Army of Darkness.*"

SCREAM

BY

STEVEN SHEA

Writer/Director/Photographer

Abyssmal, Film FestEvil, 2:22, Hoodoo For Voodoo

Instagram: @Abyssmal Twitter: @StevenShea

StevenShea.com

I was 15 years old when *Scream* was unleashed to the unsuspecting masses. I grew up on an island in the Florida Keys, where the tiny theater near us never got first run movies. Luckily, home video thrived, and I found myself hanging at the local video store, often renting VHS tapes and begging for posters when they were tearing them down. I was a total '80s slasher kid, staying up late at my great-grandma's house to watch her uncensored HBO after she fell asleep. That's where I first discovered the world of horror. My cousins were into sci-fi, *Star Wars, Flight of the Navigator,* and whatnot. I couldn't care less, as I was addicted to the thrill of survival flicks.

I remember the details of my first viewing of *Scream* like it was yesterday. It was spring of 1996, and my friend had told me that there was a new horror movie I just had to see, one that would blow my mind. I thought that was a pretty tall order and welcomed the challenge. I mean, my mind doesn't get blown that often. His dad had rented this new slasher movie from the director of *A Nightmare On Elm Street* (which I was a huge fan of). We sat on his white couch on that frustratingly humid Florida afternoon and watched *Scream*. Every few minutes he would ask me, "Who do you think the killer is?" He giggled to himself because he already knew. I would have a new character every time. I really couldn't pinpoint it, and the guessing game kept me on the edge of my seat. Utilizing all of the '80s slasher tropes to my advantage, I felt I had a pretty good idea of who I thought it would be, and then was completely flabbergasted to discover the truth. This movie did actually blow my mind. Yet strangely, I felt like I was at home in it. These characters acted exactly like my friends and me, they talked like us, made pop culture references like us, and were really into movies like us. The idea of a film being self-referential was mind boggling to me at the time. It opened up a totally new mindset about cinema. I had always loved movies, but it wasn't until *Scream* that I realized there is a whole handcrafted world behind them. Back then, you didn't have DVDs and easily accessible special features. You would have to catch a special on TV to learn about what happened behind the scenes. It didn't really sink in that there was actual thought put into films until viewing this movie. I don't know why it hadn't dawned on me - as if these flicks just popped into the universe or something from a Hollywood portal. I never looked at movies the same way again.

Scream turned my vision of horror on its head. It had that fresh, out-of-the-oven feeling; something familiar, but fantastic. There was no question that Ghost Face was en route to being the newest horror icon, and the huge wave of copycat slashers that followed proved just that. Wait, so you are telling me that the telephone, the device you use to communicate with people and call for help, can suddenly work against you? This movie turned answering the phone into the same horror that *Ghoulies* did for toilets. Never had I seen a who-done-it where they tell you who the slasher is off the bat, but in such a way that you immediately strike him from your potential-killer-list, because obviously the writers wouldn't dangle that in front of you so easily right? Wrong. Then the idea of TWO killers, working together? Impossible. Not to mention, setting up rules and then breaking them. How many times does this movie just make you second guess yourself? It's not insane, it's incredibly smart! Kevin Williamson's writing gave the teen audience a respect that we didn't know we deserved. Up until that point in horror, I felt like slasher movies were more about who could have the higher creative body count, than really making the audience think and solve the puzzle.

I was a very big fan of the movie *Psycho* (who isn't) and the hidden references and similarities in *Scream* really shined through to me. The superstar Hitchcock blonde first kill, the character names and line references, it was all amazing, even referencing *Halloween*, to the point of actually watching it in the movie! This elevated the film to this whole other place of self-awareness. Wait, are movies allowed to reference other movies? Is Hollywood real in movieland? This concept was totally alien to me and almost felt wrong at the time. And similar to *Halloween*, in *Scream* the weapon of choice is a knife. It wasn't a chainsaw or giant machete, it was an item that pretty much every household in America has on hand. How could something so simple and readily available cause so much chaos? It was terrifying. The horror came from every home in the country; you just need a phone, a knife and a mask. It's so simple, it's horrifying. Still, at the heart of *Scream* is initially a spoof of the pile of 1980s slashers that we cherished (ironic, since they later spoofed *Scream* with *Scary Movie*). Again to me, it felt like home.

Wes Craven has always been the director whose style I most tried to replicate, and I continue to do so in my career. The way he brought in simple, everyday elements and twist them to become a threat was superb. Whether it was dreams, road trips, telephones or people living under your stairs, he always had such control of his craft. It was consistently mesmerizing.

Plus, can we talk about the soundtrack? Building off of Marco Beltrami's incredible score from the simple piano to the heightened strings, to the chaos of sounds and the chorals; it builds what feels like a brand new mood of tension and unease. Mixed with the perfect track of "Red Right Hand" by Nick Cave and the Bad Seeds, the musical settings are superb. I'm so much of a fan that when my wife Melanie and I got married, our first dance was to Gus' cover of "Don't Fear The Reaper" from the soundtrack. Just perfect.

This to me was the flick that made me want to become a filmmaker. It showed me the delicacy of the craft, and really pulled back the curtain on the industry. I was inspired in a way that I didn't know was possible. I immediately immersed myself in the field. I got a job at my local video store, (because in reality I WAS that Randy character). I got hired at a TV station to learn cameras and editing. I worked at a movie theater to learn how film projection worked. This film really jump-started everything for me. I still watch it consistently and every time it's almost maddening how good it is. But hey, we all go a little mad sometimes.

FRIGHT NIGHT (1985)

BY

RYAN TUREK

VP of Development/Producer
Halloween (2018), *Happy Death Day, Ma*
Instagram: @RyTurek Twitter: @_RyanTurek

It's the summer of '85. *Rambo* was an explosive drive-in experience I would never forget. *The Goonies* took me on a pirate-themed adventure evading boobie traps and criminals. *Back to the Future* introduced me to the coolest guitar-playing, skateboard-riding, time-traveling teenager ever: Marty McFly. I was nine years old and I had not fully been activated as the living, breathing horror fanatic I am today. That changed, however, in early August when Tom Holland's *Fright Night* graced the screen. Yes, my favorite horror movie of all time is indeed my first theatrical horror movie experience. The good news is, my selection isn't driven by nostalgia that might be blinded to a film's flaws that get glaringly worse as it ages. *Fright Night* is as energetic and clever now as it was that fateful night I was taken to see it.

Allow me to set the stage for my first viewing experience. Apologies if you've heard this before, it's my first time recounting it in print.

"Horror" was a curiosity to me at the age of nine. I had read some scary comic books and maybe caught - through my own mischief - a sliver of something terrifying or two on television. (A version of *The Hound of the Baskervilles* and the birthing scene from *Humanoids from the Deep* are seared into my brain.) A horror movie on the big screen was completely foreign to me, so, on a Friday night my father tells me we're going to the movies. We hop in the car and set off for the theater - it's anyone's guess which one, but I know it wasn't in my hometown of Wallingford, CT. As we crossed through the center of town, we hit a stop light and my dad turns to me and says, "This is going to be really scary. Are you sure you can handle it? If not, you can hop out and walk back home."

Sidenote: You may think that was harsh, but it was a different time then. I was a free-range child. Those kids from *Stranger Things*? Yeah, that was me. So making the trek back home on foot through the woods and backyards was nothing.

I took a beat to process "This is going to be really scary," recalled the poster tagline which read "There are some very good reasons to be afraid of the dark," and accepted the challenge. My father smiled and we continued on our way. Needless to say, *Fright Night* was really scary! Well, to my nine-year-old self, of course.

For those uninitiated with this "Boy Who Cried Vampire" tale, William Ragsdale plays Charlie Brewster, a sexually frustrated teen who discovers that the new neighbor next door (Chris Sarandon as the charming Jerry Dandrige) is a creature of the night. Protecting this bloodsucker during the daytime hours is Dandrige's housemate (?) - a calm, creepy Renfield-type named Billy Cole (Jonathan Stark). Poor Charlie's girlfriend Amy (Amanda Bearse) doesn't believe him. His pal "Evil" Ed (Stephen Geoffreys) humors him with vampire protection tips, but doesn't believe him either. Charlie has nowhere else to turn but to local TV horror host Peter Vincent (the incomparable Roddy McDowell) and the more these two desperate, unlikely vampire hunters meddle in Dandrige's affairs, the more Charlie puts those he loves in harm's way.

Brimming with '80s style, assured direction and performances and a myriad of awesome practical FX, *Fright Night* quickly found its way into my heart (I still get chills when I hear the opening of Brad Fiedel's track "Come to Me"). When I was young, I wanted to be both Charlie and Ed; strong enough to overcome my fears but also be willing to embrace the weird stuff Ed loved. This reaction to the characters was due to a tight script written by Holland. Fright Night seamlessly blended the teen angst formula that was so prevalent in the '80s films I was responding to with classic horror storytelling tropes I had not yet been familiar with. This beautiful fusion of new and old had me stepping out of the theater craving more contemporary horror and had me eager to look at horror films of the past that informed *Fright Night*.

Since that '85 opening night screening, I've seen *Fright Night* countless times (VHS, laserdisc, DVD, Blu-ray...). I've studied it and worked it into my talks with filmmakers as an example on how to blend tone (the film is more horror than comedy, but humor is such an integral part of it) and weave solid character arcs. An original folded one-sheet hangs in my home (I'm staring at it as I write this). Needless to say, the love for *Fright Night* is strong.

I remember declaring one day in film school, "If they remake *Fright Night*, I'm just going to quit any aspirations of working in this business!" Well, that was put to the test in 2011 when Sony decided to update the movie. Obviously, I'm still here - my film school self was maybe being a bit irrational - and my thoughts on the remake are best reserved for when you and I, dear reader, meet in-person. But there you have it: my favorite horror film. Now, before you say, "What about *Halloween*? Or *Scream*? WHAT ABOUT THOSE OTHER TITLES YOU TALK ABOUT SO MUCH?" Well, a lot of great horror films fall into other categories for me. *Fright Night* is something special, hitting me at just the right age and setting me on a path that loves the macabre with a dash of playfulness.

BLOW OUT

BY
BROOKE LEWIS

Actress

iMurders, Kinky Killers, The Mourning, Slime City Massacre, Dahmer vs. Gacy

Instagram/Twitter: @BrookeLewisLA

When the topic of "my favorite horror movie" arises, there are a few things my friends and fans know about me. I'm a cinematic thriller junkie, a total '80s girl (Have you seen my big hair? LOL!), and a proud Philly Chick, so it seems fitting for me to share my favorite Brian De Palma horror/thriller, *Blow Out.* While most young girls dreamt of growing up wanting become Meryl Streep in *Silkwood*, I dreamed of growing up and playing Nancy Allen as Sally, the "hooker with a heart of gold," in *Blow Out.* Those dreams came true when I played Nicole in *Slime City Massacre* and Maura in *Sprinkles.* It's scary how the Universe works, huh (wink)?

As soon as we got our first VCR, it was like, "Stick a

fork in me, I'm done!" (pun intended!) and my obsession with horror and thriller films began. I was naturally obsessed with the 1980s greats, including *Friday the 13th* and *Prom Night*, but soon discovered an affinity for mystery thrillers like Hitchcock's *North by Northwest* and *The Birds*, and even more obscure mystery thrillers like (my idol) Elizabeth Taylor's *The Mirror Crack'd*. Clearly, I was an old soul as a young girl. Then one day, my Mom and I went to the video store (yes, I am dating myself!) and rented *Blow Out*. My Mom loved John Travolta and I was so excited to watch a movie that was filmed in my hometown. (I still get excited when I watch *Blow Out* and pick out all the famous locations and historical sites like the Liberty Bell, Reading Terminal Market and City Hall!).

Although my Philly pride has always been a big part of my love for this film, there were many other components that struck a cinematic chord in me and made me fall in love with Brian De Palma's work and direction. As seen in many classic Italian films, De Palma creates a film noir feel for the viewer with his artistic use of varying red colors. Of course, he delivers his famous split-screen shots, which have been seen in his most notable films like *Dressed to Kill*, a technique Staci Layne Wilson and I also used in *Psycho Therapy*...(shameful plug, I know). He also imitates a bit of film art from one of my other favorites, Alfred Hitchcock, in the scene that became one of the De Palma's most iconic shots of his career, in which Jack (John Travolta) tears through his studio to search for the audio recording through an extended 360-degree revolve. I still get vertigo every time I watch this! Additionally, De Palma uses music composition to create another character, dramatizing the intensity of the car accident and kills in the vein of Hitchcock's *North by Northwest*. Lastly, there is the script and writing I have come to love, repeating De Palma's themes of including sex, adultery, violence, guilt, paranoia and obsession...all components of a fantastic, classic whodunnit suspense picture!

If you have not seen this classic, and you are a true horror fan, De Palma offers so many reasons to love *Blow Out*. The basic premise of the film revolves around Jack (Travolta), as a master audio technician who makes his living recording sounds for B horror movies. (You love it already, don't you?) One night he is out recording sounds for a film when he witnesses an accident in which a car swerves through a guard rail and into a river. Jack jumps in to help and finds the driver dead, but he manages to save the passenger, Sally (Nancy Allen). He soon finds out that the driver was the frontrunner in the upcoming presidential election, and, after listening to the recording, he suspects this was no accident. There are several plot and character twists, including the understated and brilliant performance John Lithgow gives as Burke, the corrupt government's gun for hire, later revealed to be a total psychopath posing as a serial killer, the "Liberty Bell Strangler," during Philadelphia's historic Liberty Day Celebration. A horrifying scene with Burke traumatized me for life, creating a lingering fear in me whenever I enter a restroom with stalls. (I am not kidding!) Here, Burke devises another kill to make it look like a serial killing and follows a Sally look-alike hooker into the restroom at Philadelphia's 30th Street Station. The restroom has a row of stalls and, as she stands in the stall, Burke looks down from above in the adjacent stall, piano wire in his hands, waiting for that exact moment to strangle her to death and cut her throat! To this day, I look up and around the entire time I am in a bathroom stall, especially if I am alone in the room! Adding to this talented cast is veteran actor great, Dennis Franz, who plays Manny Karp, the smarmy, scheming photographer responsible for bringing Sally into the blackmail set-up.

Now...my Sally! As an actress, who had the title "Scream Queen" bestowed upon her many years ago, I am honored to have been inspired by incredible actresses from the '80s, including icons like Nancy Allen, Jamie Lee Curtis and Adrienne Barbeau to name a few! I love that these women take pride in all genres they have acted in, and that Nancy Allen proudly calls herself "The Scream Queen!" As I mentioned earlier, Sally was a role that I yearned to play when I grew up. My acting coaches and inspirations have always taught me to gravitate toward roles that have my essence, and I feel like Sally is one of them. She is sassy and mouthy with that Philly grit, but also has a heart of gold and would never intentionally hurt anyone. And, that accent! Oooo...I freakin' LOVE it! (Do you hear a lil Ms. Vampy in Sally? LOL!) The viewer can so easily fall in love with her character, as I did, and this is part of the reason the gut-wrenching ending is so powerful and painful!

That said, let me quickly address and acknowledge the genius in both the opening and closing scenes of Blow Out. The opener immediately grabs your attention, as we see Jack working on a B horror movie in a low-budget film post-production studio, watching the horrific footage of an actress about to be killed in a shower scene, and she has the worst "Scream Queen" scream we have ever heard! So, they audition other actresses to dub the scream. This is truly genius and hilarious on De Palma's part! Then, without too much spoiler, there is the famous ending that stabs like a knife in my stomach to this day! Even though I know the ending, I still feel like that viewer who roots for Jack to get to Sally in time! And, the brilliant closing scene...dubbing..."Now that's a scream!"

WES CRAVEN'S NEW NIGHTMARE

BY

THOMMY HUTSON

Screenwriter/Author/Director/Producer

Jinxed, The Id, Truth or Dare,

Never Sleep Again: The Elm Street Legacy

Twitter: @ThommyHutson ThommyHutson.com

"When the story dies, the evil is set free."

Those haunting, revelatory words are spoken by writer and director Wes Craven—playing, well, writer and director Wes Craven—in his self-referential and half-eponymous 1994 film. The phrase echoed in my head when I first heard it, but would ultimately become something of a rallying cry for me after the credits rolled.

Like most kids, I loved the movies. All kinds. Well, almost all kinds. The not-so-secret I have mentioned to some—now you—is that I didn't watch horror films at a young age so much as horror films were thrust at my I-think-I'm-ready-oh-God-I'm-not-ready little boy eyeballs. It really started with my grandmother forcing me to watch Salem's Lot with her. Actually, watch is an understatement. I was in the room, eyes covered, heart racing at every scream and screech and music sting. It continued with my brother sneaking me in to see An American Werewolf in London. (My God, what was I thinking?)

But it wasn't until Wes Craven's *A Nightmare on Elm Street* that I saw the true terror of the movies. I was never the same since and knew, at that moment, I would be a filmmaker.

The problem was there weren't many (read: zilch) opportunities to learn, do, and be filmmaking in small town Upstate New York. So, I did what every enterprising, budding cineaste does: I saved over a thousand dollars, bought a VHS camcorder, and made my own movies. Those gems still exist somewhere. I pray they remain unfound.

Craven's original creation, a serious, horrifying, in-the-shadows evil (the specter of Krueger is only in the film a mere eight minutes), went on throughout five sequels to become a part of the mainstream: a slick, wise-cracking, MTV anti-hero that had his burnt visage on everything—it would seem—but cereal boxes. This was Hollywood after all, and in Hollywood, the voice of the box-office is louder and more convincing than anything in even the best screenplay.

As time went on, and the films became more and more fantastic, audiences waited less for the kill than for the wisecracks Krueger would use. This was not the character Craven had dreamt up. And, honestly, it was not the Krueger who stuck in my little boy mind, forcing me to confront my own fears while simultaneously setting me on a quest to fulfill my dreams. I was going to make movies. I was going to meet Wes Craven.

Fast forward. Picture it: Hollywood, 1994.

It's been said that it is a town where nobody knows anything. I'm not here to argue that point, but I feel confident in saying that Wes Craven did know his audience. He understood what made them tick, often winding them up so tightly they (we) became desperate to explode in, pardon the pun, nightmares and screams.

And the time had apparently come for Craven to right the wrongs done to his Nightmare creation. To bring his Krueger back from the dead, if you will. The funny thing was, as planned as that aspect was on the part of he and Bob Shaye, it was absolute happenstance that I even saw the film when it came out. I'm glad I did because it changed my life.

I had only recently arrived in Los Angeles to attend UCLA. I didn't have a car, a job, or family nearby. I traveled thousands of miles across the country with just two suitcases of essentials: clothes, toiletries, books, and some Fangoria magazines. Tucked away in one of those beloved issues (#97, with Tom Savini's *Night of the Living Dead* remake on the cover, if memory serves) was a return plane ticket home. Just in case. One day after a particularly early accounting class I was on a bus I didn't normally take, on an unusual route, contemplating doing that just in case thing: using the airline ticket home, this time to stay. I realized I needed to figure out where I was and where I was going.

Literally.

I stepped off the bus and looked up into blinding sunlight. I was in front of a movie theater, the now long gone Hollywood Galaxy General Cinema on Hollywood Boulevard. It loomed over me as I readied to contemplate crushing my own dreams. As my eyes adjusted to the light I noticed something on the marquee that both confused and invigorated me. Four words, one title—

Wes Craven's New Nightmare.

Now, be aware this was before the internet was a big thing. I was nowhere near being one of the 1 in 10 Americans online. I didn't have a television. No newspaper subscription. And, in the interest of full disclosure, I had not bought or read a Fango since my move. (I know, I know…)

The bottom line was this: I had no real idea what this *Wes*

Craven's New Nightmare was. But, I knew I had to see it.

I moved into the theater lobby and power-walked to the poster.

That brow. Those eyes. It's—is that—Freddy?

Oh, dear Jesus, Heather Langenkamp is in this?

And Robert. Englund!?

This is a freaking *Elm Street* movie!

In my mind I ran around the theater screaming and waving my hands as if I were a teen girl at a Backstreet Boys concert. This unknown-to-me *Nightmare on Elm Street*, written and directed by Wes Craven and starring Heather Langenkamp and Robert Englund, may not have been a burning bush, but this was prophetic significance.

I bought my ticket, grabbed a box of Raisinets, buttered my popcorn, and sat down in the auditorium. In my giddy excitement, where I suddenly felt like the kid waiting for the original *Elm Street* to start a decade ago, it barely registered that I was the only one in the theater. This screening, this message, this herald, was meant for me and only me.

I'm not here to recount the plot of the seventh *Elm Street* film. (Though I will argue it is the best of the sequels by far). What I will say, however, is that it is scary, fascinating, ironic, moving, and powerful. From Heather Langenkmap playing "Heather Langenkamp" to Wes Craven offering a plausible reason for the horrors inside the movie and, by extension, our own world, *Wes Craven's New Nightmare* constructs a wonderful sort of cognitive dissonance— a horror movie about the effect of horror movies on people who make and watch horror movies.

Oh, and then there's Freddy. But this is not Jokey Krueger. In fact, it isn't even the dream killer from the 1984 classic. It's a distillation as much as it is an augmentation of the dark forces that swirled within that entity Craven brought to life. A new and intoxicating black magic elixir of evil forces that can all-too-quickly get out of control. New makeup, new outfit, new glove. A fifth razor claw on the thumb. All the better to slash at you, my dear. It worked for me in more ways than I can count.

I also understand that, for many, it did not. There are those who feel the film is too cerebral for its own good. (To that I say thank you, Wes.) Some complain Freddy is barely in it. (Like the original, his minimal screen time is a punctuation.) The makeup is weird, the costume is different, the actors are playing themselves, talking about their past, where is Nancy, and on and on and on. I've heard them all and have had plenty of healthy debates with its detractors. Looking back, I now know the fact that I was the only one in the theater was a sign, less of my wants and desires, and more of the power of a less-than-stellar box-office.

Wes Craven, though, was a very smart man. And, yes, *New Nightmare* is a very smart movie. And, like most Wes Craven movies, what made the film work on a deeper level for me was that the more I watched (and I watched it a lot) the more I started to see myself and the trials I had to go through. I didn't need to dry swallow sleeping pills to save my child, but I did need to wake up. I wasn't running for my life on a freeway, but I almost decided to run away from my goals. I needed to figure out and defeat my own demons of self-doubt and find a way to not let them get the better of me.

It was proof for me that Craven's films weren't simply scary movies. They were much, much more. Truthful, compelling, and when they worked, prescient. *New Nightmare* is no exception, as we would all see just two years later with a little movie called *Scream*.

Wes was always able to find a way to say something in an interesting and innovative way. Love, hate, or indifference aside, *New Nightmare* is no different. As a fan of both horror and country music, I like to say that Wes Craven was meta when meta wasn't cool.

For me though, watching those new nightmare images unfold truly was my watershed moment. I, like the characters in the film, had to come to terms with what I thought Freddy was, what he became, and what he was going forward. But also how to understand and, eventually, conquer it. The thing. The unexplained voice of darkness and doubt that lurks within us all reaching up from the depths to drag us down, down, down. In a sense, it forced me to think of my own trajectory into adulthood—what I wanted, what I set out to do, and how I was going to make that happen. It began to feel as heady as the film, but that was one of the things I loved about it. It made me think about more than what was unraveling on the reels of celluloid. This wasn't just a movie about Freddy or Heather or Wes. This was, as Heather reads from the script she finds, "her life." Mine, too. The tagline, "This time the terror doesn't stop at the screen," suddenly seemed to mean a lot more.

Of course, movies can be, and mean, many things, but *New Nightmare* found its way deep into the psyche of viewers and had them (me) asking a question way beyond the norm of, "Was it scary?" or "How did it make you feel?" No, this film by master of horror Wes Craven had me (all of us) asking a very different, though no less fascinating question: could a movie ever truly be dangerous. It's an important question from a writer and director who had been known throughout his entire career to ask the important questions. He just couched them in scares. He knew how to get us where we lived. We couldn't hide from Freddy if he was always in the back of our minds. And everyone has a Freddy. Mine was whether to stay or go.

Because I happened upon a film I didn't know existed, from a writer and director whom I admired, I stayed in Hollywood. If Wes Craven could reinvent his own creation I could certainly reinvent my way of thinking. It might not be easy, but neither was Heather fighting Freddy in a hellish netherworld. And, hey, that turned out pretty okay. No matter what came at me, I was ready to put up one hell of a fight. I was going to answer the call to play my own Nancy one last time.

The film has had a lasting, incredible, tangible impact on my life, professionally, personally, and creatively. Wes Craven and his *New Nightmare* inspired me in 1994 and continue to do so today. It set my life off in a new direction, one that led me to being a writer, producer, director, and creator. I got to meet Wes Craven. My path has intersected with more than a few *Elm Street* cast and crew. Without a doubt my life and career are all the better for it and I am even luckier that I can call many of these people friends.

Like the man himself, *Wes Craven's New Nightmare* was intelligent, fresh, bold, and had something important to say. I am glad I listened. I would not, could not, let my story die. Because I saw the film I followed my dreams. To have done anything less would have been, you guessed it, a nightmare.

Thank you *Wes Craven's New Nightmare*. I owe it all to you.

CRITTERS

BY
JORDAN DOWNEY

Writer/Director/Producer
The Head Hunter, Techno Western,
Critters: Bounty Hunter, ThanksKilling
Twitter: @JDowney_Film Instagram: @JordanDowney
Jordan-Downey.com

I'm not alone as I write this. In fact, there's a small creature covered in fur with a mouth full of teeth sitting on my desk. It's called a Krite, and it's from my favorite movie of all time, Critters.

Practically speaking, the puppet on my desk is from a short film I made based around the *Critters* franchise, but we'll get to that later, because my love for these movies began many years prior...

Critters is the first movie that made an impact on me. Timing is important, and I happened to be around four or five years old and living on a farm very similar to the film's setting. I don't remember the first time I watched it, but I'm fairly certain it was the memorable cover art of a giant, walking *Critter* that drew me in. My older brother, Mike, had hundreds of movies on VHS and a large collection of black and white mini movie posters that he would clip from newspapers. My parents didn't outlaw horror films, but they certainly weren't encouraging it quite yet at four or five. I'd sneak into my brother's room and flip through the pages of his movie poster scrapbook, and occasionally pop in one of the tapes. This is how I first discovered *Critters.* Of course, you don't know at the time what kind of an effect a random movie may have on your life, but looking back, I can honestly say it changed everything.

The movie scared me, absolutely. I was terrified of small creatures lurking in the barn, in the vents, or the attic. The smaller things always got to me more because of their ability to hide in all the cracks and crevices of our old farmhouse. And yes, I connected very much to the story. I was just as adventurous as the adolescent hero Brad Brown (Scott Grimes), playing with slingshots and fireworks myself. We had a chicken coop and animals on the farm just like in the movie. The fog would drift through the fields no different than what was on-screen and my Dad had a similar old shotgun which would have been our only source of protection against a monstrous threat. My mind was running wild with how scary - yet fun - being caught in an alien invasion may be. But what ultimately made me feel safe, and the one element that really cemented my love for this movie is the bounty hunters.

Faceless heroes from outer space coming to save the day — that's f*cking cool! "Get the bounty hunters!" is my favorite line from the movie, and I acted that quote out more times as a kid than I can remember. I loved the transformation scenes, and I loved the subtle relationship developed between Ug (Terrance Mann) and the boy Brad. There's a moment at the end of the film when Brad looks up to Ug and says "I just wanted to say...thanks". Ug smiles, hands him a gift, and walks off. It's so simple, but says so much. This, and the family dynamic at the core of the movie, are the keys to making *Critters* truly special.

It has heart, it takes itself seriously, and it's not mean spirited.

Now as much as I love the first film, the three sequels each made their mark on me as well. I'd bet I actually watched *Critters 2* more times as a kid than I did the first film. It's bigger, with more monsters and destruction, and really takes all the creature gags to another level. It's probably the one casual *Critters* fans remember more fondly. *Critters 2* expands the scope to the entire town of Grover's Bend, Kansas, which drove my Dad mad because I had him hunting for this town, thinking it existed in real life. At the end of *Critters 2*, there's a title card that reads "The producers wish to thank the people of Grover's Bend," so naturally, as a kid I figured it was a real place I could visit. My Dad travelled to Kansas City for work and would ask around if anyone had heard of this town, but I think deep down he knew I was on a wild goose chase. Funny enough, years later in Los Angeles, I talked my way into a horror awards show and told this story to Mick Garris, the director of *Critters 2*.

Critters 3 came at a point when I was firmly a mega fan of the series. It ends with "To be continued," and I had to ask my parents what that meant. When they explained that there must be a fourth one on the way, I must have gone insane trying to figure out when *Critters 4* would be released. When it finally arrived a year later, it was rented out at my local video store, so I had to open a new membership at a different store called Purple Cow Video just to get it. I was heartbroken to see the series end there, but if anything, it only made me ask the questions that led to me becoming a filmmaker.

Critters was the first movie that made me love cinema. It made me wonder how movies were made, where they were filmed, and how cool it must be to simply be a part of it all. When I started making my own short films, I would use bits of music from the *Critters* soundtrack and clips of spaceships landing as cutaways. I studied the series on IMDB and learned that a director was different from a writer. That interest kept growing and took me to film school in Los Angeles, where I tried to cast actors from the *Critters* series in my student films.

Lin Shaye even personally called me back to say she was busy, but it was one of the kindest and most thoughtful phone calls I've ever received to this day. The puppet watching me write this is from a five minute *Critters* fan film I directed called *Critters: Bounty Hunter*, which is really where my adoration for this franchise and my career as a filmmaker merged. The short was met with love and support online and from fellow fans of the series. Just recently, I lit up when producer Barry Opper mentioned our short on one of the *Critters* Blu-Ray commentary tracks. On another occasion, I spent time with the Chiodo Bros. who were more than generous in talking with me and showing me some of the props from the movies. These experiences have meant the world to me because at one point, it all seemed so impossible.

I feel very fortunate that I discovered what I wanted to do at a young age. Of course it's partly thanks to many movies, but *Critters* is the one that will always be special and the movie I proudly say is my favorite. In many ways, nothing has changed since I was a kid. Outer space, monsters, science-fiction, and horror are still what drive me to this day. The puppet sitting on my desk is not only a reminder of where I've come from, but also inspiration for where I want to go. What I've learned from this is that, no matter what a movie's genre or subject matter may be, there's an audience for it and there's a strong chance that your work might make a bigger impact than you think. So if ever there's a time to say it, it's now — THANK YOU, to every cast and crew member who worked on the *Critters* series. I hope you know that the time, energy, and effort you put into these movies has not gone unnoticed. Kill more Krites!

EVIL DEAD II

BY

CURTIS RX

Composer/Writer/Director

Creature Feature, Rufus Rex

Instagram: @Curtis_Rx Twitter: @CurtisRx

There's a certain point in your life where all of your interests just happen to line up perfectly and you discover something that feels like it was made specifically for you. The story of my favorite horror movie starts with a trip to the Gold Mine arcade, built to look like an actual mine shaft in my small hometown mall. Any free time and money that I could scrounge up was always spent playing the latest arcade games with the other obsessed kids, who were also depleting their weekly allowances and fistfuls of quarters carefully dug from between the sofa cushions.

On one particular day, when I had already blown through all my spare change, I started my long trek across the mall and back home. I always chose a specific secret, creepy, concrete corridor hidden off the beaten path. It was like something pulled straight out of George Romero's *Day of the Dead*. I would always daydream different zombie scenarios while making my way towards the light at the end. Luckily for me, this corridor (a glorified fire exit) was on the same path as Sam Goody, the now-deceased video and music store chain. This just also happened to be the same day that they were changing out the posters in their displays for some of the upcoming movie releases for the local theater.

As I stood there, rationing the last few sips of my cherry Icee, my attention was drawn to the newest poster for a film which I knew absolutely nothing about. The poster was mesmerizing. It had a towering castle in the background, a horde of reanimated skeletons, miniature human doppelgangers using a fork and matches as weapons, a square-jawed hero standing on an overturned car, and a damsel in distress clinging to him. As if that wasn't enough amazing imagery to throw onto a poster, the hero also had...a chainsaw for a hand. The poster for Sam Raimi's *Army of Darkness* was the coolest image I had ever seen.

From that point on, it started a new obsession. What was the deal with this weird movie? How could I find out more about it? Somehow, after mentioning the poster to everybody I came in contact with, and scanning countless back issues of *Fangoria*, I stumbled upon my answer. It turned out that *Army of Darkness* wasn't just a stand-alone movie, it was actually the third in a series of films. I didn't have to wait several agonizing months for this movie to be released, there were already two other movies in this trilogy and I could go watch them immediately.

I instantly rode my bike to our local video rental store and scoured through the horror section on the hunt for the previous two movies. I had no luck finding the first *Evil Dead*, but they had one lone copy of *Evil Dead II* sitting on the shelf. The all-black VHS box had nothing but a skull staring back into the depths of my soul and the sparse title written in blood red. How had I never seen this cover before? How did this film elude me for so many years? I quickly scooped it up, paid the fee, and rode back home.

Now, up until this point, horror was always my go-to genre of choice, but I hadn't really obsessed about any movie yet or felt the need to watch anything more than once. Normally, I just watched it, enjoyed it, and moved onto the next one, devouring them as quickly as a plate of Totino's Pizza Rolls. This is exactly why, when anybody asks what my favorite horror film is, it's an easy answer that I don't even have to think about. My favorite horror movie will always be *Evil Dead II.*

The second I pressed play on the VCR, *Evil Dead II* was everything I wanted in a horror film but never even knew I was looking for. It was a perfect combination of everything I already loved. It was *The Three Stooges* meets a comic book meets a video game meets an isolated haunted house in the woods. Unlike most of the slasher, zombie, or realistic horror films I saw before this, I had no clue where *Evil Dead II* was taking me and where it would eventually drop me off during its runtime. Spoiler alert, it takes you on a journey with a bumbling nobody en route to a cabin in the woods and drops you off with a larger-than-life hero with a chainsaw for a hand magically transported back to A.D. 1300 as the prophesized "Hero From The Sky."

From the moment *Evil Dead II* begins, it prides itself in not conforming to any of the real world logic that most horror movies try to adhere to by making the fantastical parts feel somewhat grounded. Once a series of ancient words are recited from an abandoned reel-to-reel tape recorder, every single scene that follows is an unexpected surprise, a new outlandish turn of events. It is weird horror at its finest. I'm sure we've all seen this movie an unfathomable amount of times by now, but when you sit down and just think about all the strange stuff that goes on, it's pretty unbelievable. All the severed limbs, the gallons of blood, and the bizarre fever dreams blending the lines between horror and comedy happen in only eighty-four minutes. It's an insanely perfect, live action horror version of a blood-splattered *Looney Tunes* cartoon that ends in a place that nobody in their right mind would have ever guessed.

Story and plot aside, there's an amazing technical side to *Evil Dead II,* too. The film is like an hour and a half intensive film school course. With its use of strange camera angles, dizzying movements, POVs from the myriad of evil entities roaming the woods, scenes shot in reverse, optical printing, and undercranking, the film is transported from the real world into a dreamlike spirit world untethered by any sort of logic we've become accustomed to.

Before watching *Evil Dead II,* I never paid much attention to any of the technical aspects of filmmaking, but after a single viewing, I wanted to know everything I could about it. I needed to know more about all the weird camera angles, lighting, set design, baffling camera stunts, and all the special effects that seemed to defy logic.

Not only did *Evil Dead II* instantly become my favorite horror movie, it also inspired me to start working on stories and films of my own. I put together a group of friends from school, made them watch the film, and then we started making our own little horror movies on a cheap camcorder that I put on layaway at Circuit City. I started writing horror scripts, learning how to construct makeup special effects, and reading every book I could find on low-budget filmmaking. If I wasn't watching a horror movie, then I was researching them.

The first film I ever made was a complete rip-off of *Evil Dead II.* It wasn't very good at all, but it couldn't have made me happier. I recreated the flying eyeball gag. I made my own version of the Book of the Dead with strategically placed duct tape that slowly opened the book as if it was moved by invisible hands. I toiled for days to create the perfect Karo corn syrup fake blood and equally disgusting green demon bile. I learned how to make plaster molds, candy glass bottles, and cast breakaway plates, all because of watching *Evil Dead II.*

As the years went on, my short films, stories, and ideas began to move from ripoffs, to homages, then finally to something entirely my own, all inspired by the film that started it all. It's an understatement to say that *Evil Dead II* made an impact on me and put me on my particular path in life. It was my crossroads moment and I dread to even think of what my life would've been like if I hadn't discovered this crazy little horror film.

I could go on for days and days about *Evil Dead II*, but that's exactly how you should react when somebody asks what your favorite horror film is. You should respond with an overabundance of praise and a flood of never-ending stories about it, then you should find like-minded friends, pool your knowledge, and create your own things that someday might trigger the same response in others.

MY FAVORITE HORROR MOVIE
SCREAM TEAM:

Christian Ackerman has produced over 20 feature films including *Slayer: The Repentless Killogy*, *Portal*, *Deadly Reunion*, *Bethany*, *Family Vanished*, and two *Stalked By My Doctor* films. As a director, his shorts *Hell's Belles*, *The Summoners*, and *Watch Your Back* have won over 35 film festival awards.

Felissa Rose came to fame as the star of the iconic *Sleepaway Camp*. Since then, she has produced and/or starred in dozens of films including *Victor Crowley*, *Stalked By My Doctor: A Sleepwalker's Nightmare*, *Killer Rose*, *Hanukkah*, *Return to Sleepaway Camp*, *Slayer: The Repentless Killogy*, and *Terrifier 2*.

Chuck Foster is a screenwriter and journalist who co-wrote *The Summoners* and *Watch Your Back*, a featured segment of the *1000 Zombies* anthology. He has contributed to *The Big Takeover*, *Under the Volcano*, *The New York Waste*, *HorrorGarage.com* and, most recently, *Film Threat*. Also a musician, he records and performs in the horror film-influenced synth band Pide Ayuda with his wife Jen Foster (to the occasional roar from his cat Smokey) in NYC.

Designer Josh McKevitt has featured work on several film and TV shows such as *American Horror Story: Cult*, *Perry Mason*, *Bliss*, *Vida* and *The Mindy Project*. One of his many hobbies includes practising prosthetic makeup FX on himself, which led to creating the *My Favorite Horror Movie* cover mascot, Uncle Crusty. He currently resides in Los Angeles with his fiancé Gabrielle and their Welsh "Terror" dog, Lemon.

Printed in Great Britain
by Amazon